REAL
COMMON
SENSE

For Fran + Tim —

*Engaged citizens
of the world.*

love,

Bri   *5/11*

REAL COMMON SENSE

USING OUR FOUNDING VALUES
TO RECLAIM OUR NATION AND STOP
THE RADICAL RIGHT FROM
HIJACKING AMERICA

Brian Kahn

Seven Stories Press
NEW YORK

Seven Stories Press
140 Watts Street
New York, NY 10013
www.sevenstories.com

College professors may order examination copies of Seven Stories Press titles for a free six-month trial period. To order, visit http://www.sevenstories.com/textbook or send a fax on school letterhead to (212) 226-1411.

Book design by Jon Gilbert

Library of Congress Cataloging-in-Publication Data

Kahn, Brian.
 Real common sense : using America's founding values to reclaim our nation and stop the radical right from hijacking America / Brian Kahn. -- 1st ed.
   p. cm.
 ISBN 978-1-60980-126-7 (hardcover)
 ISBN 978-1-60980-367-4 (ebook)
  1. United States--Politics and government--2009- 2. Tea Party movement.
 3. Social values--United States. 4. Values--Political aspects--United States.
 I. Title.
  JK275.K34 2011
  320.51´30973--dc22

                              2010048513

Printed in the USA.

9 8 7 6 5 4 3 2 1

We hold these truths to be self-evident, that all men are created equal, that they are endowed by their Creator with certain unalienable rights; that among these are Life, Liberty, and the pursuit of Happiness.

—DECLARATION OF INDEPENDENCE, JULY 4, 1776

We the People of the United States, in Order to form a more perfect Union, establish Justice, ensure domestic Tranquility, provide for the common defense, promote the general Welfare, and secure the Blessings of Liberty to ourselves and our Posterity, do ordain and establish this Constitution for the United States of America.

—PREAMBLE TO THE CONSTITUTION OF
THE UNITED STATES

Our situation is piled high with difficulties, and we must rise to the occasion. As our case is new, we must think and we must act anew. We must disenthrall ourselves, and then we shall save our country.

—ABRAHAM LINCOLN, 1862

We need to do a better job of teaching good old-fashioned patriotism—just that sense of loyalty and obligation to the community that is necessary for the preservation of all the privileges and rights that the community guarantees.

—GENERAL DWIGHT D. EISENHOWER, 1943

CONTENTS

DEDICATION

Tom Paine's pamphlet, *Common Sense*, was published in January 1776. America's free population was 2 million. Within three months, 100,000 copies were sold. Paine was a fierce champion of the political, social, and economic rights of the common man, and the book ridiculed the idea central to the rule of kings—that some men, because of bloodlines, or inherited position, had the God-given right to rule. The book galvanized the Continental Congress and the nation in support of the cause of national independence. On July 4, our nation's Founders signed a document that changed the course of history.

In 1792, Paine wrote *The Rights of Man, Part II*, in which he blamed the European monarchies for poverty, illiteracy, unemployment, and war. He called for basic reforms—representative government, public education, relief for the poor, pensions for the aged, public works for the unemployed, and a progressive income tax to pay the costs. The British government banned the book, jailed its publisher, and indicted Paine for treason.

Today, America's extreme Right is trying to re-write our nation's history, and deny our Founders' commitment to social justice. As part of that effort, pundit Glenn Beck has gone so far as to steal the legacy of Tom Paine, using *Common Sense* as the title for a book—and praising Paine. But the book itself attacks the very ideas in which Paine believed, and if the great patriot were alive today, Glenn Beck would label him a radical socialist or revolutionary Marxist.

This book is dedicated to Tom Paine—patriot, visionary, and American Founder.

INTRODUCTION

We face unprecedented challenges, as a people, a nation, and a world. Can we humans—amazingly inventive, psychologically complex, personally flawed, and not yet very wise—pull together and do what needs to be done?

Yes, we can.

But doing that will require important changes in our personal and national priorities, in the structure of our economy, in the integrity of our government, and in how we invest our nation's resources to achieve our goals. Achieving these changes in turn depends on a basic shift in *values*. This book argues that the values we need are the very same ones on which our nation was founded—the ones that led to the best in our past; the ones that will light the way to a worthy future for our children and theirs.

In 2005, when I began to develop the outline of *Real Common Sense*, the state of our nation looked fine to America's economic, political, and media elites—the economy and stock market were strong, and our country's global dominance seemed uncontested. But I saw something else: Forty-five years of the Cold War combined with a decades-long credit binge had taken our nation far off course. We were adrift in a sea of consumer goods, our priorities increasingly set by a globalized economy and soulless media promoting instant gratification and quick money as the dominant purposes of life. Politicians, pundits, and well-financed "think tanks" championed "The Ownership Society," where private wealth and material possessions were more important than shared community values and the public good. Internationally, in the aftermath of 9/11, we accepted the dangerous illusion that our security could be assured by ourselves alone—through overwhelming military power, unquestioned belief in our moral superiority, and inexhaustible wealth.

I first outlined the concepts in this book in a speech in Miles City, Montana, a part of the country where the word "neighbor" is still used as a verb: "We neighbor." The truth is that we humans all "neighbor"—we give and receive mutual support to and from each other. But modern life camouflages that truth, and as a result we suffer the dangerous illusion that we are *independent* of each other. People around Miles City still say "we neighbor" because their lives remain tied to the production of food from the earth, visible interdependence, and a living sense of community. As they struggle to cope with economic globalization and hard times, they will need that awareness, and will need to act on the basic American values of human equality, personal responsibility, and common purpose that underlie our still young national experiment. If they do, they have a fighting chance to reshape and revitalize their town, their region, their human community.

We, the people of the United States, also have a fighting chance.

It will not be easy. Almost all of us are tied to the consumer economy. Every day, through all kinds of media, we are encouraged to think of ourselves as *consumers* instead of as *citizens*. The consumer "frame of reference" is private, individual, and reinforces the "illusion of independence" from each other and from our community. In doing that, it undermines our commitment to the unique legacy and challenge left to us by our nation's Founders: our democratic Republic committed to liberty and justice for all.

Each of us sees what life has taught us. I grew up in the 1950s and '60s among rural people, in the family of a writer who had been blacklisted during the McCarthy era. I was taught that all people have intrinsic worth and basic rights; that a central part of the human story is the struggle to see that value honored, those rights achieved—not just in words, but in the living world.

I was lucky to be born in America, a nation that at critical points in its history has led the world in that struggle. My life has exposed me to a diversity of people. I was raised in a farming community, went to college and law school in cities; I've worked as a ranch hand, college boxing coach, lawyer, politician, film maker, conservationist, and radio journalist. I've worked with cattle ranchers and members of the corporate elite, prisoners and corrections officers, artists and carpenters, loggers and environmentalists.

Over time, I have learned that some of what I was raised to believe was naïve or oversimplified, or simply wrong. But the basic values I was taught—grounded in the decency, honor,

integrity and deep heart of everyday people—have been reinforced again and again. And I have come fully to believe that
the *never-ending pursuit of a better world*—where the worth,
rights, and responsibilities of every person are honored—provides each of us, and our human civilization, the moral
compass and direction we need.

On July 4, 1776, our nation's Founders gave us the lodestar
for that compass: *We hold these truths to be self-evident, that all
men are created equal, that they are endowed by their Creator with
certain unalienable Rights; that among these are Life, Liberty and
the pursuit of Happiness.*

This book discusses the construction of America's moral
compass over time—by the Founders, visionary leaders, and
everyday citizens; how powerful interests have ignored,
opposed, and tried to undermine it—and still do today; and
how, by rediscovering that compass to navigate the dangerous
and uncharted waters of our time, we can find our way forward
as a people and nation, and leave a future worthy of our grandchildren.

Brian Kahn
Helena, Montana
November 2010

CHAPTER I

WHERE WE STAND

Our situation is piled high with difficulties, and we must rise to the occasion. As our case is new, we must think and we must act anew. We must disenthrall ourselves, and then we shall save our country.

—ABRAHAM LINCOLN, 1862

The time has come to reaffirm our enduring spirit; to choose our better history; to carry forward that precious gift, that noble idea, passed on from generation to generation: the God-given promise that all are equal, and all deserve a chance to pursue their full measure of happiness.

—BARACK OBAMA, 2009*

The purpose of this book is to remind us of the essential moral compass the Founders bequeathed to every citizen so that we can put it to use to resolve the major challenges we now face.

▪ The global and national economy is failing to meet basic human needs. Since 2008, our economy has teetered on the brink of collapse: 7.8 million jobs have been lost since the start

---

* This book uses quotations of Barack Obama as presidential candidate and president. Clearly, many Americans believe his presidency has not lived up to the promise of his words. Whether that is due to the balance of power in Congress, the depth of the economic crisis, failures of leadership, or other factors is a matter for another book. He is quoted here because his words echoed key beliefs of the Founders, and his use of them inspired the American people.

of 2008,[1] and more than 2 million homeowners faced foreclosure proceedings in 2008 alone.[2]

- In 2010, 14.6 million people were officially unemployed, another 5.9 million had stopped looking for work, and 8.5 million worked part-time but wanted full-time work—a total of almost 30 million Americans.[3]

- Next to China, our nation is the world's largest contributor to global warming—a threat that, if not reversed, jeopardizes the lives of the generation of children being born today.

- We are by far the richest nation in world history, yet one in seven of our fellow countrymen—43.6 million people—live in poverty, including one in five of our children.[4]

- Another 57 million Americans are near poor, earning between $20,000 and $40,000 a year. They are one divorce, one injury, one illness away from financial disaster.[5]

- The gap between the wealthy and the working middle class is the widest in the developed world. In 2007, the wealthiest 25 percent of Americans owned 87 percent of the nation's private wealth. The top 1 percent owned 34 percent and received 23.5 percent of total income.[6] In 2009, the top twenty-five hedge fund managers "earned" an average of $1 billion each. A worker earning $50,000 a year would need to work 20,000 *years* to make that much money.[7]

- Corporate giants make millions selling damaging junk food to our kids. Eighteen percent of teens aged twelve to nineteen, 20 percent of children aged six to eleven, and 10 percent of children aged two to five are obese.[8]

- More than a quarter of American children live in single-parent families.[9]

- Our prison population exceeds 2 million people—the highest prison population rate in the world—not including people in county jails or on probation or parole.[10]

These realities exist despite an increase in the gross domestic product from under $5 trillion in 1980 to $14 trillion in 2007.[11] During the same period, national economic policy was dominated by "free-trade" globalization, "pro-market" privatization, and "free-market" deregulation. Ronald Reagan played a central role in the emergence of these policies, and famously enunciated their underlying premise: "Government is not part of the solution; it's part of the problem." Since 1980, through every means of modern communication, that message has been driven home by the American Right:

- Government is wasteful, inefficient, and interferes with the private sector, the creators of wealth.

- Get government out of the way and we'll all be prosperous.

- It's your money, not the government's.

- Cut taxes for corporations and for the well-off, deregulate the banks, and they will create high-paying jobs.

- Let "free trade" and "free markets" rule, and the economy of America and the entire world will prosper.

In 2008, this philosophy produced the starkest economic crisis since the Great Depression—uprooting the middle class and undermining the opportunity for which America is famous.

Yet proponents of these policies call themselves "conservative." (See Appendix for the definitions of the political philosophies discussed in this book.)

Webster's Dictionary defines "conservative" as "tending to preserve; inclined to keep up existing institutions and customs; moderate, cautious." My grandfather was such a man. His ancestors fought in the American Revolution, his grandfather in the Civil War. He took pride and believed in the traditional American values of family, hard work, initiative, frugality, personal responsibility, and integrity. His handshake was better than any contract. He believed in private property and free enterprise, along with bedrock responsibility to the community of which he was a privileged member. He worked hard, took care of his family, was engaged in his community, and gave generously to charity.

Today, "free-market" think tanks, columnists, and commentators insist that selfishness and greed are virtues, rather than vices. To them, the most admirable social goal and highest achievement is to make as much money as you can, as quickly as possible. Wherever profit-driven markets lead is fine, whether it is selling junk food to kids, putting sleazy sex on family TV, hawking blood-spraying violence through video games, spilling toxins into drinking water, raising executive salaries at the cost of working-class jobs, or encouraging unmanageable credit card and home mortgage debt. Hiding behind "conservatism," the reactionary Right is trying to turn profit-driven markets into a universal religion.[12]

My grandfather, a genuine conservative, rejected all that. He knew that such "principles" had nothing to do with honorable conservatism. To him, *earning* wealth quickly was impossible: Honest, fast money was a contradiction in terms. He understood greed for what it was. He was a religious man and knew that every major religious leader from Jesus to Mohammad to Kung Fu-Tzu deplored it.

And so did our Founders. They believed that responsible citizenship required much more than the exclusive pursuit of self-interest. In the 1850s, Abraham Lincoln engaged in a series of debates with the pro-slavery politician, Stephen Douglas. In Peoria, Illinois, Lincoln drew "a line in the sand," saying that slavery would go no further; he tied slavery directly to the blind pursuit of self-interest, a direct attack on the nation's founding values:

> I hate [slavery] because of the monstrous injustice of slavery itself. I hate it because it deprives our republican example of its just influence in the world . . . and especially because it forces so many really good men amongst ourselves into an open war with the very fundamental principles of civil liberty—criticizing the Declaration of Independence, and insisting that there is no right principle of action but *self-interest*.[13]

In 1936, President Franklin Roosevelt said: "We now know that greed is not only bad morals. It is bad economics."

Yet today's grim state of our nation and the world has only emboldened the reactionary Right—unscrupulous politicians, hate-mongering pundits, ideology-driven "newscasters," and Tea Party leaders.

The need for serious reform of the global corporate economy is dismissed with contempt as unpatriotic, "un-American."

In fact, it is they who are un-American: Rather than return to our real Founding principles, the Right extols predatory concepts of "natural selection" and economic inequality, trumpets a free market fundamentalism packaged as "economic liberty." It has no concern for human consequences, and, most fundamentally, denies the right of the people's government, in the words of the our Constitution's Preamble, "to promote the general Welfare."

In the face of our nation's problems, many of us feel that all we can do is complain. Which brings to mind a story:

A devout young man joined a religious order in a monastery where he took a vow of silence, under which he was allowed to say one word for each year of successful service—one word for the first year, two for the second, and so on.

At the end of his first year he came for his audience with the Father, who said, "My son, you have successfully completed one year of service. Do you have anything you would like to say?"

The young man opened his mouth, pointed to an upper left molar and said, "Hurts."

He was sent to the clinic, his badly abscessed tooth was removed, and he returned to his duties.

At the end of the second year, the young man came for his audience and the Father said, "My son, you have successfully completed two years of service. Do you have anything you would like to say?"

The young man pointed to his shoes and said, "Too . . . tight."

He was sent to the commissary and given a proper-fitting pair of shoes. His infected blisters healed and he resumed his duties.

At the end of his third year the young man came for his audience and the Father said, "My son, you have successfully completed three years of service. Do you have anything you would like to say?"

The young man said, "Want . . . to . . . quit."

"I'm not surprised," the Father replied. "You've done nothing but bitch since you came here."

And the alternative to bitching?

The alternative is to think clearly, to orient ourselves, and to act.

I boxed in college and learned the hard way that when you encounter serious adversity you better have the fundamentals down. For our nation, the fundamentals are the principles on which the United States was founded. It was a moral compass bequeathed to us by the Founders—great, visionary men. Men who had lived under the dictatorial rule of aristocrats and religious dogmatists. Men who had studied the great Greek, Roman, and French philosophers and had shared the Enlightenment's bedrock faith in human reason, human dignity, and the worth and equality of all human beings. That is why, when they came together in the summer of 1776 to declare independence from the greatest empire in the world, they used these words:

> We hold these truths to be self-evident; that all men are created equal, that they are endowed by their Creator with certain unalienable Rights; that among these are Life, Liberty and the pursuit of Happiness. That to secure these rights, govern-

ments are instituted among Men, deriving their
just powers from the consent of the governed.

It is true that the Founders were imperfect men. Many did
not believe that women were their equals; in the nation they
established, women would not obtain the right to vote for
more than a hundred years. Many did not acknowledge the
humanity and rights of Native peoples. Terribly, some of the
Declaration's signers themselves owned, bought, and sold
human beings as slaves. Thomas Jefferson recognized the fundamental contradiction between what he believed—that all
men are created equal—and how he himself lived as an owner
of slaves. He wrote that no one could participate in that slave-
owning system without becoming "depraved."[14]

Despite these tragic truths, the Founders were able to artic-
ulate a vision of democracy that would launch American
history on an unprecedented trajectory toward greater freedom
and justice. In the Declaration of Independence, in the Preamble to the United States Constitution, and in the Bill of
Rights, they enshrined principles that have, in Lincoln's words,
given "hope to all the world, for all future time."

Was Lincoln right? As Americans, in our heart of hearts,
we know the answer. It is to these principles, these profound
moral values, that we citizens of the American Republic must
look, and act on together, to secure a worthy future for ourselves and future generations.

CHAPTER 2

WHERE WE'VE BEEN

*They are the two principles that have stood face to face from
the beginning of time; and will ever continue to struggle.
The one is the common right of humanity, and the other the
divine right of kings. . . . It is the same spirit that says, "You
toil and work and earn bread, and I'll eat it." No matter in
what shape it comes . . . it is the same tyrannical principle.*

—ABRAHAM LINCOLN, 1858

Change is difficult for us humans because it threatens our most basic sense of who we are. Each of us forms that personal sense within the world as we come to know it, the world of our childhood and youth. The more rapidly things change during our lives, the sharper is the conflict within us: Are these changes good or bad? Do popular new public values mean that the ones I hold dear are wrong? Am I out of date, irrelevant? How can I get my bearings in this new, evolving world? What should I hold onto from my own past? What should I let go? What should I embrace or reject from the new?

To explore these questions of today we need to understand our past: We cannot know where we are, or where we are headed, unless we know where we have been.

Our human species is approximately 200,000 years old—

roughly 8,000 generations. For 190,000 of those years we lived in small groups of twenty to thirty souls, obtaining our living directly from the natural world. We hunted animals and birds and gathered wild fruits and vegetables. We developed a sophisticated ability to work together—hunting large and dangerous animals, caring for our tribes' children, defending our territory, and surviving in harsh climates. *We did these things together and evolved these cooperative skills because our species' survival depended on it.* There were no "rugged individualists." Punishment for chronic bad behavior was exile from the community. It meant certain death: No individual could survive alone.

Though much has changed in our physical world since our hunter-gatherer past, we remain human beings, biologically and psychologically. We are the same capable people who were able to survive Arctic winters with stone tools and animal-skin clothes, who developed the sophisticated skills needed to build boats, sail vast distances, migrate across continents, and adapt our ways of living to vastly different climates. We are the same human beings, and carry within each one of us that profound array of capabilities, inclinations, weaknesses, and strengths, the same capacity to hate and to love.

Some 10,000 years ago we began to domesticate plants and animals, a seemingly simple act that profoundly altered our existence. Our sources of food and shelter became fixed in location; we produced and stored surplus crops and built towns, then cities. Society became stratified, leading to a pyramid of economic and social classes: the mass of serfs, slaves, and peasants at the bottom and a tiny, all-powerful aristocracy at the apex. These rulers demanded worship of gods who conveniently ordained the rulers' power—"the Divine right of Kings." Such governments served wealth. In the words of the eighteenth-century Scottish philosopher Adam Smith, "Civil government . . . is in reality instituted for the defence of the rich against the poor."[15] United States President John Adams was more succinct: "Power always follows property."[16]

During most of the 10,000 years of feudal aristocracy, the concepts of human rights, human equality, and human progress were unimaginable. But the period did lead to important steps forward: written language, recorded documents, great cities, and the flowering of art. What we now call "civilization" has lasted roughly 400 generations.

The development of the Industrial Age began roughly 300 years ago, a mere twelve generations. With dramatic suddenness, the possibility emerged to liberate human beings from backbreaking labor and reform the rigid feudal system. The power of the aristocracy-Church dictatorship began to crack. In the late 1600s—spread by word of mouth and the stunning new technology of easily printed books—the radical concept of the Enlightenment raced around the world: Human beings are rational, and in their capacity to reason lays their full potential; morality arises from the innate compass in every human, and is determined by reason—not dictated dogma. The new philosophy maintained that every human had inherent worth; every person had natural, God-given rights by virtue of being a human being; using reason and science we could improve the conditions in which we lived; and those improved conditions would enable us to live more moral, civilized, meaningful lives.

The American Revolution was the dramatic product of this

Enlightenment philosophy, and our Founders were Enlightenment disciples. The values they championed, fought for, and died for were Enlightenment values.

In 1776, a mere nine generations ago, our nation was founded. Abraham Lincoln described it in the Gettysburg Address: "Conceived in Liberty, and dedicated to the proposition that all men are created equal."

Yet the Founders were divided over slavery—the forced conversion of millions of human beings into private property to be bought and sold, bred like animals, used for forced sex and labor. Jefferson and his allies attempted to have slavery banned under the new Constitution. But others disagreed. Men who identified themselves as Christians quoted the Old Testament's support for slavery and labeled those who urged its abolition as subversives, anti-property-rights radicals, and "anti-Christ." It was not the first time, nor would it be the last, that financial self-interest would blind otherwise principled people to the most fundamental moral truths.

Seven decades later, on his inauguration as vice president of the Confederacy, Alexander Stephens baldly stated the pro-slavery case:

> (The Confederacy) is founded on exactly the opposite idea (from that of the Declaration of Independence's principle of human equality); its foundations are laid, its corner-stone rests upon the great truth, that the negro is not equal to the white man; that slavery—subordination to the superior race—is his natural and normal condition.[17]

The failure of political leaders to confront slavery and their decades of moral equivocation in the face of the immense profitability of that system permitted the subjugation of millions of people, and led, in 1861, to 600,000 American deaths in the Civil War.

It took more than a hundred years from the Civil War's end—through the Voting Rights Act of 1965—to achieve for every American a basic element of equality—the right to vote. In four human generations, America changed fundamentally. From a rural farming economy we developed into the largest industrial nation in the world and became global leaders in engineering, manufacturing, and international finance; we emerged from the Second World War as the most powerful nation on earth, our economy more than twice that of the Soviet Union. And after more than four decades of the Cold War, in 1991 the United States of America emerged as the sole superpower. In all of human history, no nation has achieved comparable global dominance.

Having reached such heights, we should be providing for all the needs of our people, and looking forward to decades of peace and prosperity.

Yet less than twenty years into the "Age of the American Empire" that is not what we now face. Why?

In 1946, Albert Einstein wrote: "The unleashed power of the atom has changed everything save our modes of thinking, and we thus drift toward unparalleled catastrophes."

We can amend that: Atomic power *and everything else that we've developed in the last sixty years* has changed everything, except our way of thinking.

In Thomas Jefferson's time, nothing moved faster than the speed of a horse. Ideas, commerce, information, armies. It took weeks for a letter to go from New York to London; it took another month for it to reach Moscow. Today communications and transactions of all kinds are instantaneous, and the economic and social consequences are immense. In this new super-speed world, all economic things are intimately tied together in an interactive chain. In 1920, if Mexico's banking system had been threatened with collapse, the impact would have been entirely local. But when that happened in the early 1990s, the world economy shuddered. American investors and economists argued that the US economy was at risk, and demanded—and got—a multi-billion dollar bailout of the Mexican banks. In the first decade of the twenty-first century, Chinese need for copper, cement, steel, and petroleum skyrocketed—and economies around the world confronted higher commodity prices. In 2008, the price of oil went over $140 a barrel, straining economies worldwide.[18] Greed-driven investments in American sub-prime mortgages and toxic derivatives led to a global collapse of stock markets and an international recession. *Economically, the world is more fully interdependent than ever before.*

This interconnectedness extends beyond the economy. When AIDS emerged, modern transportation enabled it to spread around the globe with astonishing speed. Carbon dioxide produced by Russian, American, and Chinese coal-fired power plants and gas-guzzling cars warms the earth's atmosphere, changing climate everywhere. The t-shirts and sneakers we wear are often manufactured under harsh conditions on the other side of the globe. The far lower living standards in these countries encourages millions of people to migrate in search of a better life; desperate, they take poverty-level jobs in developed nations and become pawns in polarizing, anti-immigrant politics. The threats of social, economic, and environmental upheaval are no longer simply domestic concerns—they are shared globally.

Ultimately, the interdependence of today's world means that the privileges and living standards of any one nation's citizens are tied as never before to the living conditions—and good-will—of all the world's people.

Wealth and power encourage people to believe that their security and welfare is *independent* of others. This illusion is potent and blinding to individuals, communities, and nations. It has recently led America to exaggerate our power, our ability to act alone, our control over events. To take just one example: Political and military leaders, ignoring centuries of Middle East history, believed that the "shock and awe" of American weapons would produce easy victory and a wave of Arab democracies in America's image. The result: hundreds of thousands of dead and wounded men, women, and children; 4,400 American soldiers killed; one trillion dollars diverted from needs here at home; inflamed anti-American feeling around the world; and, according to the 2006 US Intelligence Estimate, a new global recruiting bonanza for Al Qaeda terrorists.

In the real, interdependent world, the illusion of independence has consequences.

CHAPTER 3

CITIZENSHIP AND COMMUNITY

We the People of the United States, in Order to form a more perfect Union, establish Justice, ensure domestic Tranquility, provide for the common defense, promote the general Welfare, and secure the Blessings of Liberty to ourselves and our Posterity, do ordain and establish this Constitution for the United States of America.

—PREAMBLE TO THE CONSTITUTION OF THE UNITED STATES

That we here highly resolve that these dead shall not have died in vain, that this nation under God shall have a new birth of freedom, and that government of the people, by the people, for the people shall not perish from the earth.

—ABRAHAM LINCOLN, Gettysburg Address, 1863

The Preamble to the Constitution was drafted in the summer of 1787 and adopted by the delegates to the Constitutional Convention. The Founders wrote the Preamble after their failed first attempt at a national government, the "states' rights" structure of the Articles of Confederation. The illusion of "independent" states had proven disastrous, and so they cited as their first purpose "to form a more perfect Union." They understood that the states were *interdependent*, and that only by pulling together could our nation thrive.

The very next purpose was "to establish Justice." Thomas Jefferson would later write that "exact and equal justice for every man, irrespective of station" was the most vital principle for democratic government. This principle was grounded in the Founders' central assumptions about human beings, the American people, and civic life. They shared the belief, dating back to the Greek philosophers, that a sense of civic duty on the part of *each citizen* was the bedrock of civilization and democracy. *The Founders believed that each American was a free citizen in a community of citizens. And that every citizen, and the community at large, had interdependent rights and responsibilities.* Thus, American citizenship and the American community are the unique and precious inheritance of every American.

The interrelationship is pivotal: Citizens cannot exist without community—they are *of* community. And a democratic community must have free citizens pursuing personal, human fulfillment and simultaneously willing to devote a portion of their time, thought, and energy to public purpose. John Adams, perhaps the most influential member of the first Continental Congress, and later the second president of the United States, summed it up this way:

> The end of the institution, maintenance and administration of government, is to secure the existence of the body politic; to protect it; and to furnish the individuals who compose it with the power of enjoying, in safety and tranquility, their natural rights and the blessings of life. . . .
>
> The body politic is formed by a voluntary association of individuals. It is a social compact, by

which the whole people covenants with each citizen, and each citizen with the whole people, that
all shall be governed by certain laws for the
common good.[19]

Despite the Founders' vision, American culture has over
time come to emphasize the role of the individual and over-
look the critical role of community. I host a radio program.
When I interviewed historian Stephen Ambrose, author of
Undaunted Courage, the best-selling account of Lewis and
Clark's Corps of Discovery expedition, he said that, in his view,
much of our emphasis on individualism arose from the delayed
publication in the nineteenth century of Captain Lewis' journals. As a result, the centrality of *teamwork* to the successful
exploration and expansion of the nation—as exemplified by
the mutual support and self-sacrifice of the Lewis and Clark
expedition's members—was hidden. In its place emerged the
romantic, attractive myth of the rugged individual taming and
settling the American West. "Hell," Ambrose said, "the West
was settled by groups of people working *together*."

The myth gained power during the late nineteenth century
as vast individual fortunes were accumulated by men at the
apex of the economic pyramid. A classic example was The Big
Four, key investors in the development of America's transcon-
tinental railroad network: Leland Stanford, Mark Hopkins,
Charles Crocker, and Collis Huntington. The endeavor, essential to the development of our nation, received huge
government subsidies through the Pacific Railway Act of 1862,
which gifted to the railroads ten square miles of public land for
every rail mile built and guaranteed the investors needed funds

through government-issued bonds.[20] The engineering that was required to achieve this phenomenal feat was carried out by hundreds of design and construction engineers. And the years of backbreaking, pick-and-shovel labor was done largely by tens of thousands of immigrant Chinese laborers working under the harshest conditions.

But in terms of national mythology, The Big Four emerged as "self-made" men who on their own became titans in railroads, banking, shipping, and politics—instead of talented and fortunate individuals who amassed stunning fortunes through government subsidies and decades of work by tens of thousands.

That romantic and potent myth of the rugged individual—in today's terms, the "individual entrepreneur"—has a profound impact on American public policy. It influences who among us is considered to be "productive," worthy of government subsidy, to what extent wealthy individuals and businesses are taxed, and what wages workers earn.

In his first message to Congress in December 1861, Abraham Lincoln said:

> Labor is prior to, and independent of, capital. Capital is only the fruit of labor, and could never have existed had not labor first existed. Labor is the superior of capital, and deserves much the higher consideration. Capital has its rights, which are as worthy of protection as any other rights.[21]

That historical perspective has been forgotten, and very few American politicians would dare today to echo Lincoln's view. As a result, when Massey Energy has 1,342 safety violations over five years, and twenty-nine miners are killed in an explosion, the owner of the mine remains a free and wealthy man.[22] And when investment bankers' greed and fraudulent investment vehicles take the nation's economy to the edge of a cliff, hundreds of billions in taxpayer funds bail them out. They even get billions more in bonuses, while millions of wage earners lose their jobs and homes.

The point here is not that entrepreneurship and the investors of capital are unimportant: They play a key role in the dynamic of our national and international economy, and should be rewarded and incentivized. But the fact is that the implementation of entrepreneurial ideas—and the subsequent generation of wealth—depends on an intricate, living community, including our public schools that create an educated workforce, taxpayer-funded subsidies, public transportation and roads, a host of other publicly supported institutions, and, most fundamentally, the whole community of people who do the actual work. That truth should be reflected in our daily lives, in the rewards everyday people get for the hard work they do, in the quality of the education our children receive, in medical care, and in the financial security of old age that every citizen deserves.

AN ARMY OF ONE

Our exaggerated emphasis on the role of the individual is revealingly reflected in the way that the United States government has recruited young Americans to join the armed forces. From 2002 to 2007, the United States Army recruitment slogan was "An Army of One." When the new theme was announced, the *New*

York Times reported that it had been developed by an ad agency exactly like a consumer product, with alternative slogans tested in focus groups. Of all the slogans evaluated, it provided the most effective appeal to today's individualistic and consumer-oriented young person. The "target audience" was clear when I watched the "Army of One" recruiting video. It was a high-voltage advertisement, seventeen minutes of fast-paced images designed like a soft-drink or beer commercial—exploiting a teenager's thirst for fun, adventure, sex, and personal power.

What's wrong with that?

What is wrong is that our nation was asking its young people to put their lives at risk based on a lie. Military service is quintessentially about *teamwork*. It is about people who work together, who risk their lives for the other members of the team, as well as for their families, their communities, and their nation. Military service is an ultimate expression of putting community above self.

This irony is not lost on those who have fought for their country.

Shortly after the slogan was announced, I asked a military recruiter what he thought.

"It is a disgrace," he said.

In 2005, I interviewed Bud Moore, of Condon, Montana. At eighty-seven, Bud was still living in a log cabin that he built with his own hands. He was a teenager in the Great Depression, running an 80-mile wilderness trap line alone, the ultimate self-reliant man. After America was attacked at Pearl Harbor he joined the Marine Corps and fought in three first-wave assaults of Pacific island beaches.

I asked him, "What did you learn as a Marine? How was

it for a young man who'd grown up as a classic, rugged individualist?"

Bud said, "I grew up thinking I lived in God's country, and that my neighbors were the best people in the world. And I still believe that in a way. But I found out there are a heck of a lot of good people out there. I learned it was great to be part of a team, part of the whole. A lot of times your life depends on the guy next to you. He might be some little guy, a feather merchant from New Jersey. But he'll come through. Always. The Marines will never let you down."

The United States Army invented its "Army of One" recruiting slogan, and advertises signing bonuses of up to $40,000, because it does not believe an appeal to good old-fashioned patriotism will "sell" to consumer-oriented teens. If they are right—if our young people have been misled and miseducated by our individualistic culture to the point where we have to lie to get them to serve their nation—we are in deep trouble.

In 1943, during the height of World War II, General Dwight D. Eisenhower, future president of the United States, wrote a letter to his brother. He said this:

> We need to do a better job of teaching good, old-fashioned patriotism—just that sense of loyalty and obligation to the community that is necessary for the preservation of all the privileges and rights that the community guarantees.[23]

That is what the Founders had in mind—*a community of free citizens*. It was for that goal, that potential, that they pledged, at the end of the Declaration of Independence, "our lives, our fortunes, and our sacred honor."

CITIZEN VERSUS CONSUMER

When we look at America's media today—media that profoundly shapes public values and opinion—how often do we hear the word "citizen" in comparison with the word "consumer"? Perhaps one time in a thousand. Why? Because in the last fifty years we have come to live in, and depend on, a "consumer economy." In 2008, *70 percent* of our nation's Gross Domestic Product was comprised of consumer spending.[24] Hundreds of thousands of businesses and tens of millions of jobs depend on this economic activity. Like all enterprises, consumer-dependent businesses want to survive and expand. And so, through advertising and other means, they promote a consumer mindset among us Americans. *They want us to act and define ourselves as consumers.* They want us to define the Founders' profound phrase, "the pursuit of happiness," as meaning the pursuit of consumer goods, happiness through the ownership of *things*. They promote their concept using every available tool, including the most potent mass media in the history of the world.

The effort is not new. Advocates of free market "conservatism" like to quote Adam Smith, who wrote extensively on the interrelationships of economics, government, and society. But Smith was in fact an opponent of blind, excessive pursuit of consumer commerce. In his 1776 book, *Wealth of Nations*, he wrote, "To found a great empire for the sole purpose of raising up a people of customers may at first sight appear a project fit only for a nation of shopkeepers. It is . . . extremely fit for a nation whose government is influenced by shopkeepers." One can imagine how Smith would have regarded today's consumer culture and profound corporate influence over government.

Does it matter how we define ourselves? Does it matter that we are told a hundred times a day that we are "consumers"? Consider this: The day after the attacks of 9/11, as we struggled to get our bearings, to understand what had happened and what we needed to do about it, the president of the United States spoke to the nation. He did not appeal to the American people in the name of the Founders. He did not call on us to pull together, to sacrifice for the good of the nation. He urged us instead to set aside fear and "go shopping." He was worried that 9/11 would disorient us so deeply that *we would stop buying*. He appealed to us not as citizens of the American Republic, but as consumers.

Yes, we are partly consumers. But we are not *fundamentally* consumers. We are first and foremost wives and husbands, parents, family members, friends. And *we are citizens in a community of citizens*.

Sixty years of TV, credit cards, and hundreds of billions of dollars worth of commercial propaganda have brought us to the point where it is vital to a "healthy economy" that we Americans see ourselves, our purpose in life, as consumers, separate and independent individuals who define our sense of personal worth by what we own, wear, and drive. That is the message driven home every hour of every day by a corporate-owned media that exists only through consumer spending.

None of us likes to admit that advertising affects us. We

like to think that our individual values and preferences determine our choices, and that commercials have no impact. If that were true, the advertising industry would be wasting the billions it spends every year. From their research, they know they are not.

Even our desire to think that we make free choices is exploited: In the words of one of the cigarette industry's most successful executives, "It is the job of the corporation to *engineer* what is perceived as individual choice."[25]

The marketing of cigarettes is a classic example. In 1900, adult per-capita consumption of cigarettes in America was fifty-four per year. By 1963, it was 4,345.[26] This stunning change was accomplished through sophisticated marketing that exploited human vulnerabilities to sell a product they knew to be addictive and deadly. The desires of men to be daring, of women to be feminine, even of children to collect celebrity cards proved a goldmine. In the early 1960s, cigarette makers sponsored prime-time cartoons—orchestrating cigarette breaks for Fred and Wilma Flintstone—and far into the nineties, advertisements featured the now-notorious animated character Joe Camel. A study published by the *Journal of the American Medical Association* in 1991 made waves when it claimed that more five- and six-year-olds could recognize Joe Camel than Mickey Mouse.

The result of this specific, unconscionable commercial propaganda is that 420,000 Americans die each year from tobacco-induced illnesses.[27]

Why do we, adult human beings, fall for such propaganda? The answer is hard to face: Each of us is both strong and weak, resistant and vulnerable to pressure and persuasion. Fundamentally, each of us carries the complex emotions, desires, and needs that comprise the human being. Consumer advertising is painstakingly designed to manipulate these qualities in a manner that encourages us to buy. Our world has increased our exposure to marketing so much that an urban dweller in America can now expect to see five thousand ad messages a day.[28] We consider it normal to eat breakfast and dinner in front of the TV, being bombarded with consumer advertising. Company logos can be found stamped onto our eggs at the supermarket and our motion sickness bags in airplanes.

In a way, what's happened is like the frog and hot water experiment: Drop a frog in hot water and he will jump out. Put a frog in cold water, and gradually turn up the heat and he will not notice the gradual increase in temperature. Until it's too late.

ADVERTISING AIMED AT CHILDREN: COMMERCE WITHOUT CONSCIENCE

The 1934 Communications Act granted permission to the new radio broadcasting industry to use the public's airwaves, provided they did so in a manner that served the public interest. The Federal Communications Commission is the federal agency charged with regulating the industry. Broadcasters must obtain licenses from the FCC, and the conditions placed on the licenses are supposed to benefit the public.[29]

During the first twenty years of TV regulation, the agency required broadcasters to set aside significant time for educational programs, public service announcements, and news and local programming. These requirements reduced profits and over time the networks lobbied successfully to have the rules weakened or eliminated.

The people most vulnerable to media manipulations are our kids. So advertisers began to target them. When running ads during children's programming was not enough to satisfy the corporate appetite for profit, someone came up with a brilliant idea: Let's make kid's programs *themselves* a vehicle for selling. Cartoon heroes began to directly market products—video games, "identity" clothes, and junk food. The cigarette-sponsored Flintstones are perhaps the most scandalous example, but the leading cereal companies—Kellogg's, Post, and General Mills—were among the first and most successful to grasp the tremendous profit potential of "integrating" programming and marketing. Cartoon heroes appeared on cereal boxes and in cereal ads. If a four-year-old falls in love with Super Hero, she will naturally want to eat the sugar-laden cereal Super Hero eats![30]

By the 1970s, concern about negative impacts on children led to FCC hearings, and the agency adopted rules placing limits on such ads. In 1977, the FCC indicated it would consider a ban on ads for sugar-laden foods aimed at children. But fierce industry lobbying and new "pro-market" appointees of the Reagan administration led to the 1981 FCC announcement that it was dropping the issue.[31]

A quarter century later, children's advertising is a $17 billion industry.[32] The most skilled child psychologists team up with marketing spin doctors to reach through the television screen and grab the minds and hearts of America's children, causing them to judge themselves and their classmates by what toys they have, what cereal they eat, what logos they wear, and what video games they play.

Advocates of "market values" see nothing wrong with this. Kids eat cereal; they make choices; advertising gives them choices; by getting their parents to buy Super Hero's cereal, the kids are stimulating the economy, generating jobs, and increasing shareholder value. Ultimately, market advocates say, it is the parents' responsibility to decide what their children eat. It's not the advertiser's fault, they say, or the junk food maker's. It's the parents' fault.

It is an argument worth considering. Certainly parents have first-line responsibility to protect their children. And in our modern world there are many dangers to protect them against—from auto traffic and narcotics to child molesters. But it is not easy for parents to protect their kids from TV ads and consumer hype. First, they are up against the billions of dollars being spent to manipulate their children; second, especially if parents are employed, it's extremely hard to prevent their kids from watching children's programs; and finally, even if parents ban TV from their homes, children will see the ads at friends' houses, in day care, at the supermarket, or in comic books and video games.[33]

It is also fair to turn the question around: *Why should America's parents have to fight against junk food advertising to protect their children's health?*

The explosion of childhood obesity in America is astounding: Eighteen percent of teens aged twelve to nineteen, 20 percent of children aged six to eleven, and 10 percent of children aged two to five are obese.[34] This epidemic has caused the recent onset of "adult-type" diabetes in kids—a medical first. It has increased the risk of heart disease, high blood pressure, and breathing problems in every child who is affected.

Unless these trends are reversed, they will cause endemic health problems and personal suffering that will generate immense costs to taxpayers, while threatening to bankrupt our health care system and our entire economy.[35]

Every society in history has shielded its children from harm. We no longer allow tobacco companies to aim ads at kids. We pass tough laws to protect them from drug dealers and child pornographers. We don't allow children to buy liquor, drive cars, or have guns. Why isn't our government willing to pass regulations to protect kids from junk food advertising? There can be only one answer: Our public officials believe that junk food profits are more important than the health of our nation's children.

The willingness to harm children reflects the essential difference between a corporate/consumer value system and one of citizenship and community. To General Mills, selling food that damages children's health is fully proper, just as to tobacco companies selling cancer-causing cigarettes is proper: It is free enterprise that generates profit and increases shareholder value. In 2005, an Institute of Medicine report found that 80 to 97 percent of the food products now aimed at children and teenagers are "of poor nutritional quality." Many children's cereals are up to 40 percent sugar. The same year General Mills' chief operating officer Kendall J. Power proclaimed, "We strongly think the products like cereal can be responsibly advertised to children. Cereal eaters, including kids who eat presweetened cereals, are getting a good start to their day."[36]

It is worth examining what circumstances generate Mr. Power's willingness to make such a statement. In his heart he knew he was not telling the truth. So why did he do it?

Perhaps like most of us he simply wanted to keep his job so he could continue to support his family; maybe he accepted that misrepresenting the truth—parroting the company line—was a regrettable part of his job. Or, to be able to look himself in the mirror, perhaps he convinced himself that "it's the parents' responsibility," or "General Mills employs thousands of people," or any of a hundred rationalizations that enabled him to avoid facing the truth that he is deliberately harming children.

We humans are very good at rationalizing—and to some extent we all do it to explain away our failings, or justify the compromise of our principles. We need to acknowledge that if we were in Mr. Power's shoes, under the same pressures, we might well do the same thing. It is essential that we understand that the willingness to damage a child's health does not originate with the spokesman, but with General Mills, with corporate and market values.

General Mills exists within an economic and legal system that virtually requires such behavior. Because if General Mills doesn't sell junk cereal to kids—and its competitors do—it will lose market share, its stock value will decline, and eventually it will go out of business. Those are the corporate economy's rules of the game. Market rules that demand corporations place profit ahead of the interests of our children, our communities, and our nation. These market realities encourage, even demand, commerce without conscience.

The 2007–08 bank debacle illustrates the principle. Bankers generated billions for themselves by making loans without adequate security. They packaged and marketed such loans to others, who made money by reselling them. Goldman Sachs went one step further—they bet against the very packages they had sold. When it all collapsed, tens of millions of Americans paid a terrible price. In 2009, 1.4 million bankruptcies were filed, and 7.8 million jobs have been lost since the start of 2008.[37] Imagine a line of people standing five feet apart—1,000 per mile. A line like that of 7.8 million people would be 7,800 miles long. It would begin in New York City, go to San Francisco, extend south to Los Angeles, cross the country to Washington DC, go back up to New York, and head west again, ending somewhere near Illinois.

The banks that caused this human devastation received hundreds of billions in taxpayer-funded bailouts, then awarded their corporate executives billions of dollars in bonuses. They were offended when President Obama criticized them and tried to stop it.

That paragraph reads like an absurd joke. No sensible person could behave in such a manner. But people did—by the thousands. They did because the rules, pressures, incentives, and values of corporate economics said it was the only way.

Citizen- and community-based values are different: Unrestrained pursuit of profit can cause serious harm, and the right to engage in business does not extend to selling products that inflict harm on other human beings. Therefore, it is the job of "the people's government" to establish rules for the conduct of business that reflect the community's conscience, to pass laws to assure private actions do not hurt others. For example, the trucking industry's profits would be higher if truckers could drive ninety miles an hour. But we establish lower speed limits to protect public safety. My freedom to drive my car as fast as I want is restricted to protect others from harm.

The failure to establish regulation of the cereal industry, or the advertising industry, or the banking industry is a failure of representative government. Instead of protecting the community and its citizens, our government has come to support the conscienceless corporate agenda it is charged with regulating.

RIGHTS AND RESPONSIBILITIES

The essential vision of the Founders was that we as citizens had fundamental rights and corresponding responsibilities. Today's political rhetoric talks a lot about rights and little about responsibility.

Liberals and progressives have historically argued for full economic, political, or legal rights for groups who have suffered discrimination or exploitation—slaves, racial minorities, children, women, low-wage workers, recent immigrants, gays and lesbians. Conservatives have argued for strong property rights, the right to engage in business, the right of public safety.

Neither group has emphasized the reciprocal responsibilities to the rights they advocate. The responsibility for groups of people who have suffered discrimination and hardship is to be, and act as, full citizens of our country; to become as informed as possible; to care about the community and be civically engaged through volunteer work or political involvement; to vote; to give their best on the job; to be strong, engaged family members. Property and business owners have the same personal responsibilities. And something else. Rights to do business and own property carry the responsibility to use those assets in ways that enhance their personal well-being *and simultaneously* benefit their community—or at least do not directly harm it.

Traditional conservatives like my industrialist grandfather fully accepted that concept. He and liberals could argue over *how* those responsibilities should be fulfilled, but they agreed on the underlying principle. Today's free market "conservatives," along with the rest of the extreme Right, reject that idea. They are not true conservatives in the American tradition. To them, business and property owners should have absolute rights, with no responsibility. As the Tea Party Patriots state in their 2010 Core Values:

> A free market is the economic consequence of personal liberty. The founders believed that personal and economic freedom were indivisible, as do we. Our current government's interference distorts the free market and inhibits the pursuit of individual and economic liberty. *Therefore, we support a return to the free market principles on which this nation was founded and oppose government intervention into the operations of private business.*[38]

Their history is false. None of the Founders believed that any segment of society had absolute rights. Only autocrats like King George claimed that—for themselves. Interestingly, the extreme Right does *not* claim absolute rights for everyday people. They accept and advocate many laws that, by definition, limit personal freedom. Absolute rights and liberties are reserved only for business enterprise.

When we see things we do not like in our government, it's easy to blame someone else. But the truth is that each of us as an American citizen shares responsibility for the situation we now face: The quality of the United States government ultimately reflects "the consent of the governed." It's time for us all to take a look in the mirror, accept responsibility, and take action.

We can start by restoring the balance between "me" and "we." Wherever you live in the United States of America, a lot of our future depends on "we." There's nothing new in that: As Benjamin Franklin said in 1776, "We must, indeed, all hang together, or most assuredly we shall all hang separately."

For all of us, "me" always will be a fully normal, central part of our world. But an exclusive "me" mindset undermines the balance believed in by the Founders: free citizens with personal freedoms enshrined and protected by democratic government, but with no individual having rights superior to the central needs of the community. Thomas Jefferson put it this way: "(A man) has no natural right in opposition to his social duties."[39]

Our most sacred freedoms are spelled out in the Bill of Rights. Yet even these have limits. In a famous Supreme Court case dealing with the right of freedom of speech enshrined in the First Amendment, the court famously said that even that vital freedom is not unlimited: A man does not have the right to shout "Fire!" in a crowded theater. In exercising my freedoms, I do not have the *right* to harm my neighbors, my town, or my nation.

The same principle applies to organizations, including the most influential economic structure of our time: the corporation.

THE CORPORATION

Corporations are legally created tools designed to stimulate capital investment to generate economic development and wealth—essential elements of social progress and economic stability. They came into their own as vehicles to finance railroads, coal and iron ore mines, and steel-making factories, the backbone of an industrializing nation. Even the largest personal fortunes were inadequate to undertake such efforts and an organizational structure was needed that encouraged investment by a great many people. To provide an incentive, corporate law granted unprecedented immunity to investors. Owners of traditional businesses are personally liable for bad debts of the enterprise, but corporate shareholders cannot be held liable for company debt, nor can they be held responsible for illegal acts that the corporation might do. The new structure was spectacularly successful in attracting investment capital and our nation has benefited in many ways. We are surrounded by a cornucopia of corporate-produced consumer goods of low price and high quality. When we become ill, most of us have access to corporate-funded hospitals and corporate-developed miracle drugs. We drive corporate-built automobiles using corporate-produced gasoline, and are insured by insurance corporations. Most of the food we eat has been grown or processed by corporations. So are the sports teams we watch on corporate-owned TV.[40]

The cumulative economic power of these corporations is staggering. Functioning in a truly global marketplace, corporate structures are involved every day in transactions totaling trillions of dollars.

Such power is a double-edged sword. For instance, the corporate drive to expand its share of the market may be accomplished by designing and producing a better product at a lower price, benefiting customers. But it can also be achieved by eliminating competitors through hostile takeovers, cutting jobs, or destroying the competition that keeps prices down. The pressure on corporations to bring down production costs may be accomplished through investment in more efficient technology; or it can be achieved by exporting jobs from the United States to countries where people work twelve-hour days for thirty-five cents an hour; or by shifting American production to a nation where toxic chemicals can be dumped into rivers, thus saving the cost of treating them.

The risk of socially harmful business choices is aggravated by basic American corporate law, under which managers have a fundamental, legal duty to maximize shareholder value. This obligation was put in place to protect investors from corporate officers putting their personal interest first. But the unintended result is that managers do *not* have a legal duty to do what's right for their workers, their neighbors, the community in which they operate, or even the nation whose laws give them unique privileges. So when there is a conflict between what benefits shareholder value/corporate profit and what benefits the community, the institutional bias of the corporation—even its legal duty—is to act for profit.[41]

This tension between the good of the corporation and the

good of the community is in some respects no different than the "me" versus "we" balancing that each of us faces throughout our lives. But there are fundamental differences in how corporations and human beings make those decisions.

First, corporations are organizations. As such, they do not live and breathe and interact one on one with other human beings. They do not develop the emotional bonds and mutual commitments that hold human communities together—bonds that provide the invisible sense of restraint, the desire to cooperate, the feeling of shared destiny and community, the innate moral compass of normal humans. In short, they have no personal conscience.[42]

Second, corporations have the ability to mobilize huge amounts of money. Carrying out their legal mandate, they use it for whatever purpose benefits the corporation. To ensure that laws are passed that enable them to maximize profits, they form Political Action Committees, and raise hundreds of millions of dollars for the campaigns of politicians who support them. They spend additional millions to lobby for pro-corporate laws, regulations and low corporate tax rates.[43]

Finally, they exercise immense power in the places where they do business: A corporation that employs several thousand people in a city or state has tremendous political influence. If such a company says it wants something, people listen. When a major employer says, "If you tighten your air pollution rules, the jobs we provide will be at risk," it is hard to resist that pressure. To do so you need a government with courage and clout. In short, you need enough public, democratic power to balance the private, corporate power.

There is something else needed for the public/private balance to work: the foundational belief that democratic government represents and protects the public good. Precisely that idea has been under attack for the last thirty years. An extreme ideology has taken root in America that rejects the very concepts of community and the public good. Its origins can be traced in part to the author Ayn Rand, whose novels portrayed heroic individuals and entrepreneurs who overcame the hindrances imposed by communities of mediocre people. Rand was a powerful advocate with an intriguing life story. Born in Russia, she left the Soviet Union in 1926, repelled by communism. Changing her name to Ayn Rand from the original Alisa Rosenbaum, she swung to the other extreme, adopting the belief that the exclusive pursuit of self-interest was the central human virtue. By the late 1940s, her extremist libertarian ideology developed a cult following among conservative intellectuals and it continued to grow through the 1960s.

In a televised 1960 interview with Mike Wallace, she summarized her core beliefs: "Each man must live as an end in himself. I'm challenging the moral code of altruism. . . . I consider it evil. . . . Self-sacrifice is the precept that man needs to serve others in order to justify his existence; his moral duty is to serve others. That is what most people are taught to believe today. That is what makes a sacrificial animal."[44]

For Rand, greed was a virtue, and the self-focused, entrepreneurial individual represented its most noble expression—a Superman. Personal, private rights were "unconditional." The purpose of society—its *sole* purpose—was to insure these individual rights. Unlike philosopher Adam Smith, who believed that the self-interest that worked well in the economy needed to be balanced by moral virtues "to restrain our selfish(ness), and indulge our benevolent affections," Rand vehemently argued against any distinction between economic and social virtues.[45] She considered the 1964 Civil Rights Act "the worst breach of property rights in the sorry record of American history."[46]

Rand's views are key to understanding today's reactionary Right: Over a nineteen-month period ending in June 2010, Glenn Beck's website contained eight favorable references to Rand. In May of the same year he argued on his show that putting "the common good" before the individual "is exactly the kind of talk that led to the death camps in Germany."[47]

Rand asserted that all her views were based on the objective application of reason, and she strongly objected to use of religion by other conservatives and libertarians to support their pro-market views. Her militant atheism generated hostility from some, like William F. Buckley, but her strident advocacy of capitalism earned her many more conservative admirers than critics, including Senator Barry Goldwater, who admired her writing and, on the floor of the Senate, echoed her sentiments: "Profits are the surest sign of responsible behavior."[48]

Over time, her influence was felt in powerful circles. In an echo of Rand, British Prime Minister Margaret Thatcher said, "There is no such thing as 'society.'" Like Rand, she believed society is simply a collection of individuals acting out of self-interest, interacting best through voluntary market transactions. The combined effect of these self-oriented actions is assumed to achieve the greatest possible good for everyone. Therefore, public regulation of private business constitutes inappropriate infringement on individual freedom and damages everyone. Seen through this ideological lens, government regulation of business is morally wrong and economically counterproductive. In sum, to the free market fundamentalists, "private" is good; "public" is bad.

Both Thatcher and President Reagan shared Rand's view that economic progress and human virtue arose from private business: As the creators of wealth, entrepreneurs are the most virtuous of people; and businesses are the most beneficial institutions. They found natural political allies among "conservatives" like economist Milton Friedman. Former Federal Reserve Chairman Alan Greenspan was a member of Rand's inner circle who for decades argued against government regulation of business and shared Rand's opposition to the 1964 Civil Rights Act.[49]

Both Reagan and Thatcher enacted massive tax cuts for business and the wealthy. According to free market advocates, these tax cuts would generate economic growth, more taxes, and enhanced wealth for all.

Then the results came in: The Reagan tax cuts reversed a fifty-year trend of reducing the gap between America's wealthiest and the rest of the nation. Ever since, with the exception of part of the 1990s, wages for average Americans have stagnated or declined, while the incomes of the top 10 percent of Americans have increased dramatically.

The tax cuts also created the largest federal deficit since the founding of the nation, *tripling in the space of eight years the amount of national debt that had taken 190 years to develop*. The same pattern was repeated under President George W. Bush: He and Congress cut taxes dramatically, and during his two terms the debt more than doubled, from $5 trillion to more than $11 trillion.[50]

After the 2008 banking collapse, a shaken Greenspan admitted in congressional testimony that his "ideology" had failed to anticipate that corporate executives might take unreasonable risks in pursuit of profit. But these disastrous results in no way dampened the enthusiasm of the "free market" advocates. For ideologues like Grover Norquist, director of Americans for Tax Reform, and self-described advocate of a "commercial republic," bankrupting the federal government through massive deficits is a good thing. "I don't want to strangle the federal government," Norquist is reputed to have said. "I just want to weaken it to the point where I can drown it in the bathtub."[51]

Yet Norquist and his allies are not being honest when it comes to federal power. Right-wing, free market "conservatives" have aggressively pursued the weakening or dismantling of governmental authority only in *specific* areas through:

- Reduced environmental protection, including regulation of mining, logging, and grazing on public lands, endangered species protection, air emissions, and industrial pollution;

- Preventing the government from using its power to negotiate lower prices for Medicare prescription drugs—at a cost of billions of taxpayer dollars;

- Reduced enforcement of anti-discrimination and worker safety laws;

- Deregulation of banks and other home lending institutions, leading to the financial disaster of 2008–09;

- Deregulation of telephone, communications, and media corporations—concentrating media ownership in a few corporate giants;

- Deregulation of electricity generation and distribution, leading to the Enron scandal of 2001 and skyrocketing energy prices;

- Weakening of food labeling, food safety, and consumer protection laws; and most fundamentally

- Squeezing government funds for central public services, from education to health care.

At the same time, they have lobbied to use and *increase* government power in many ways:

- To carve out $1.1 trillion in annual deficit-spawning subsidies and tax breaks for targeted businesses and institutions, while at the same time decrying deficit spending;[52]

- To allow warrantless surveillance of citizens;

- To allow the detention of individuals without charge;

- To enable the president to unilaterally designate any person, including American citizens, as an "enemy combatant," subject to perpetual imprisonment without access to American courts;

- To make it harder for everyday people to obtain the same bankruptcy protections that businesses enjoy—to enhance credit card company profits;

- To make termination of pregnancy a crime;

- To use government funds to pay for services provided by religious organizations; require public schools to teach religion-based creation "science" to our children;

- To tax corporate profits and investor income at a rate lower than wage-earner income;

- To advocate federal monetary and global trade policies that generate billions in profits for these same business interests;

- To advocate ever-expanding military budgets—without raising taxes to pay the bill.

In short, the aim of such "conservatives" is to weaken government's ability to regulate business and help ordinary people, while *increasing* government intervention that enhances profits, strengthens unilateral presidential power.

Reasonable people can debate the merits of these proposals and policies. But no honest argument can be made that the "conservative" agenda is about "less government."

FAILINGS OF GOVERNMENT

The centerpiece of the Right's agenda is to discredit government as a source of social action. As a result, its propaganda consistently seeks and promotes evidence of government incompetence.

Do they have a point? Certainly.

Governmental administration is often slow; it is sometimes inefficient, unimaginative, or arbitrary. Its essential purpose is to insure fair implementation of laws and regulations—not creativity. Should we constantly be looking for ways to improve its performance? Of course.

But the biggest problem with government is something the Right doesn't want the American people to notice: Far too much of it is bought, paid for, and controlled by the very interests the reactionary Right represents. And they want to keep it that way.

Secondly, many important government functions are seriously underfunded. There are not enough Bureau of Land Management staff to thoroughly evaluate the environmental impacts of applications for coal bed methane wells—so they are told to approve them anyway. Staff of the Department of Interior's Minerals Management Division are found to be literally in bed with the industry people they are supposed to regulate. Food and, until recently, mine safety inspectors have far too many businesses in their caseloads to do an effective job. And even after they got enough mine inspectors, a flawed enforcement process enables violators like Massey Coal Company to escape punishment for years.

These facts are no coincidence. They reflect the free market fundamentalists' determination to gut the budgets for public services that they see as "interfering" with the private sector. It's a double winner for them: reduce "interference" with business; then when disaster strikes—half a *billion* eggs are recalled due to *salmonella* poisoning—blame "government incompetence."

All too often, our government leaders answer to corporations, not to citizens; that is why they often ignore the issues that affect everyday people, yet very competent in the issues that affect business goals.

WHAT IS PUBLIC AND WHAT IS PRIVATE?

Most of us would agree that in every community, every society, some things are legitimate areas or public discussion and policy, while others are purely private in nature.

Let's imagine those private and public spheres as two circles:

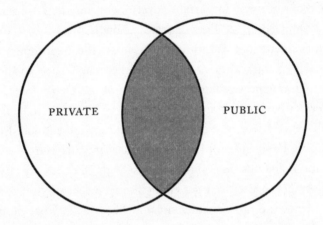

The circle on the left represents all those things that are private in our lives—the thousands of choices, preferences, values, decisions, relationships, and pursuits that go into everyday life. In this circle the public has no legitimate business.

The circle on the right stands for those topics that directly affect important community interests and values, such as clean air and water, education and health care systems, national defense, efficient transportation systems, fair enforcement of law, and access to justice. In these areas, public institutions and responsibilities are essential.

There is also a place where the circles overlap, where *both* public and private interests are involved.

An essential political debate in our time involves where private and public interests intersect, and what should be the level of public involvement where they do.

CHAPTER 4

RESTORING RESPONSIBLE MEDIA

If a nation expects to remain ignorant and free, in a state of civilization, it expects something that never was, and never will be.

—THOMAS JEFFERSON, 1816

Virtually everything the average person sees or hears . . . is determined by the interests of private, unaccountable executives and investors whose primary goal is increasing profits and raising share prices.

—BILL MOYERS, 2007

In the current model of corporate news ownership, the incentive to produce good and valuable news is simply not there.

—DAN RATHER, 2009

Television is one of the most powerful forces in the public/private "overlapping circle." It is "private" in the sense that it is run by for-profit private business, and perhaps two hundred million Americans every day make personal, private choices about what programs they watch. It is public because it uses public airwaves and it has profound public consequences. In today's world, television more than any other factor shapes public knowledge, tastes, views, attitudes, and perceptions about the larger world. Regulated by the Federal Communications Commission (FCC), the public airwaves are required by law to serve the public interest; private industry is licensed to use the airwave to generate profit.

When TV started in the 1950s, its content was seriously regulated by the FCC to assure that inappropriate sexual content was prohibited, and significant time had to be set aside for public service programs such as in-depth news. Additionally, the Fairness Doctrine required broadcasters to allocate time for discussing controversial issues, and to air contrasting views. When broadcasters' licenses came up for renewal, the FCC closely examined how well these public interest requirements had been met.

But over the decades, the television industry became a huge and profitable business and gained immense political clout. For the broadcast system to work, advertising must result in enough product sales to pay for the cost of making the ads and producing the programs, plus generate network profits, *plus* profit for the corporation advertising the products! It is an expensive proposition. Nationally, network advertising costs more than $160 billion a year.[53] Over time, the industry has lobbied for changes that would further enhance its profitability. Pro-market politicians and their appointees began to revisit a host of industry regulations and over the past thirty years have succeeded in weakening or repealing almost all the public interest provisions.[54] Additionally, lobbyists for the booming cable industry succeeded in having their industry exempted from the regulations applied to their broadcast-based competitors.

These changes have had a profound effect on the nature and

content of television programming, including what we see and depend on for our news. In essence, if a program generates enough profit we get the opportunity to see it. If not, we don't. That "profit filter" dominates all commercial TV, and has far-reaching consequences.

TV "NEWS"

Initially networks accepted that news programs were a necessary and important public service even though the expenses—reporters, broadcasters, and production—exceeded the advertising revenues they generated. But the relentless pressure to produce profits caused executives to take a second look. What if they could repackage news as "entertainment"? That change could lead to enhanced viewer ratings, higher advertising revenues, and greater profit. The result has been the conversion of formerly in-depth news to headlines, sensationalism, celebrity, and trivia.

Edward R. Murrow saw it coming: "We are currently wealthy, fat, comfortable, and complacent. We have currently a built-in allergy to unpleasant or disturbing information. Our mass media reflect this. But unless we get up off our fat surpluses and recognize that television in the main is being used to distract, delude, amuse, and insulate us, then television and those who finance it, those who look at it, and those who work at it, may see a totally different picture too late."[55]

The erosion of a dynamic free press has been exacerbated by another corporate dynamic: Rather than having an array of perspectives available on outlets owned and operated by many different companies, today just six corporate conglomerates own most of the major media outlets (down from fifty in 1982): Time Warner, Disney, Murdoch's News Corporation, Bertelsmann of Germany, Viacom, and General Electric's NBC.[56]

Bill Moyers sums it up this way: "The third pillar of democracy, an independent press, is under sustained attack, and the channels of information are choked. A few huge corporations now dominate the media landscape in America. . . . In-depth coverage of anything, let alone the problems real people face day-to-day, is as scarce as sex, violence, and voyeurism are pervasive."[57]

The truth is that almost all our information about the world is filtered by commercial corporate conglomerates. This filter—what gets through and what doesn't get through—profoundly shapes our understanding of the world, and our opinions about public policy and politics.

But the extreme Right is not satisfied with those broad filters over mass media They have taken the next step: political ideology camouflaged as news. Fox News is the most extreme example. Owned by ultra-conservative Rupert Murdoch, the channel features far Right "pundits," anchors and reactionary politicians who use the classic techniques of demagogues—inflammatory talk, fear-driving "threats" and "conspiracies," and outright fabrications. Code words and false labels discredit opposing views as weak and anti-American. Doctored videos and interviews often appear. Fox plays on racial and sexual prejudice to turn historic victims into oppressors and oppressors into victims.[58]

So Glenn Beck claims the Obama Administration is driven by "revolutionary Marxists" and that President Obama "has a deep-seated hatred of white people." Sean Hannity's website describes "the president's affiliation with radical theology, his advisers' history of Marxist activism, repression of the media, support for leftist dictators, and worse"; Michelle Malkin, who in her newspaper column called the millions of Americans who opposed the invasion of Iraq "yellow traitors," and criticized the American Civil Liberties Union for "dangerously absolutist positions against the use of torture," is selected to be a Fox commentator; and when someone criticizes Fox for leading a witch hunt, Bill O'Reilly can be counted on to accuse *them* of witch hunting. As a business model, Fox News works brilliantly.

But the concept of propaganda as news it is not new. The Nazis were masters of it. In *Mein Kampf*, Adolf Hitler outlined his plans for the seizure of power. He knew it would be essential to win over the German people to his world view, and was frank about his strategy: "The great masses of the people will more easily fall victims to a big lie than a small one." The Nazi Party worked for years to implement that principle: Their newsletters, newspapers, and speeches trumpeted big lies: Germany was the victim, not the aggressor in World War I; it had lost the war because of traitors; the German race was of "pure blood" and superior to all others; violence and war were expressions of the best in national character; socialists, communists, subversives, and Jews were parasites, sucking the economic blood of the nation and plotting to take over the world.

In the 1920s, sustained Nazi propaganda was effective in creating a committed core of fanatics. In 1928, the party received 14.3 percent of the vote. But when the hardships of the global Depression struck in 1929, the virus spread fast. In the 1932 multi-party election, the Nazis received almost 38 percent of the vote.[59] Hitler was appointed chancellor six months later, and, with the aid of his militant followers, moved decisively to destroy German democracy.

Under the rule of Joseph Stalin, mass media was used the same way, fanning public fears of economic sabotage by "enemies of the people," then using that fear to justify the imprisonment and murder of millions.

SOCIALISM AS BOGEYMAN

Like Hitler and Mussolini, extreme Right media and politicians use the "threat of socialism" as a rallying cry. But in a key respect, they are actually out-demagoguing the Fascists: During the 1920s and 1930s, there actually *were* millions of socialists and communists engaged in political battle with the fascists. And during almost fifty years of the Cold War, Marxist socialism competed with capitalism for global supremacy.

But the Soviet Union and its eastern bloc collapsed twenty years ago, and Maoist China has turned on its head. Though still under the political dictatorship of the Communist Party, the majority of its economy, now the second largest in the world, is capitalist. Rush Limbaugh, Glenn Beck, Sarah Palin, and Fox News hope that the American people haven't noticed and relentlessly raise the socialist bogeyman.

Just what *is* socialism?

Webster's Dictionary says: "A theory or method of social organization whereby the citizenry jointly owns the means of production and distribution, and the power of administrative control is vested in the state."

The concept initially gained support in Europe in the early

1800s in response to the appalling conditions forced on those who worked in the rapidly expanding industrial cities. To its followers, socialism meant the extension into the economic arena of the political equality guaranteed by democratic government. The idea gained support in the United States in the late nineteenth century for the same reasons. The prominent labor leader Eugene Debs became a socialist, and ran for the presidency four times, in 1912 receiving 915,000 votes.

During the Great Depression, with massive unemployment and the capitalist system in crisis, the socialist idea gained appeal among millions of Americans. My father was one of them. Raised in a wealthy family and attending private schools, he led a sheltered life. But traveling across America in the mid-1930s, he was stunned by the poverty he saw, the hardships and suffering of the people he met. He felt it immoral for families such as his to live in luxury while their fellow countrymen went hungry, and he concluded that the nation's wealth should be owned, shared, and managed by all the people. Even after the economic recovery following World War II, my father continued to believe that public ownership of major industries, utilities, transportation, and banks would enable full employment, housing, and education for everyone, and the elimination of poverty once and for all. Shortly before his death in 1979, he wrote:

> Today I watch the global surge of human rights.
> And as a writer let me speak of human rights not just grammatically.
> I claim the human right to live.
> I claim the human right to love.

I claim the human right to work.

I claim the right of every child to eat.

I claim the right of all to dignity of age.

I claim for every woman every right of man.

I claim each right for every shade of skin.

I claim the right of every human being to peace!

And in the dawning world, I see these rights in bloom.

In Europe and America, socialists were united by a belief in public ownership of major wealth, but divided between those who, like my father, considered themselves Marxists and those who did not. In the mid-1800s, Karl Marx had argued that historical change arose primarily from the interaction of economic and technological forces, and he emphasized the struggle between economic classes. Like pro-market philosopher Adam Smith, he believed government to be a tool of the wealthy to maintain power over the poor; he predicted that the private ownership of industrial capitalism would give way to socialism (public ownership, with wages varying according to work), which would eventually give way to communism, where government would "wither away" and people would be paid "according to their needs."

Some of Marx's followers led twentieth-century revolutionary movements in Russia, China, and elsewhere. They imposed ruthless one-party—often one-leader—dictatorships to implement socialist policies. Instead of withering away, the state became all-powerful. Non-Marxist socialists, who called themselves "democratic socialists," advocated for socialist reforms through the democratic process.

During the first half of the twentieth century, American socialists joined liberals and progressives in pushing for a wide range of reforms: elimination of child labor, mandatory public education, full rights for women and minorities, formation of unions, unemployment insurance, and Social Security.

After World War II, democratic socialist governments came to power in Britain, France, Italy, and other western European nations. (Interestingly, they remained allies of the United States in the Cold War.) Some nationalized mines, steel mills, utilities, and railroads, while the rest of the economy remained private. Conservative governments later privatized many of these industries. In Scandinavian countries, democratic socialist governments supported market economies but put in place high tax rates to fund generous unemployment, medical, and retirement benefits for citizens.

In the early Cold War years, the American Right, led most visibly by Senator Joe McCarthy, labeled all socialists as pro-Soviet subversives and disloyal. In the Red Scare and blacklisting that followed, both Marxism and democratic socialism were eliminated as political forces in the United States.

Today the extreme Right is again shouting about the "threat of socialism!" Is it true? Should Americans be afraid, and if so, of what?

Well, we actually *do* have some socialism in America.

Let's start with publicly owned land: Our federal government owns a lot it, mainly in the western part of the nation, arising from the Louisiana Purchase made by President Thomas Jefferson and from the 1848 war with Mexico. Land that was not given away to the railroad corporations, or to homesteading settlers, is largely still government-owned. Our national parks, wildlife refuges, national forests, and Bureau of Land Management lands, along with army, air force, and navy bases comprise the large majority of "socialist" land in America. And, of course, our public schools.

The free market fundamentalists hate public ownership of land, precisely because it is "socialist." In the west, there are regular calls for the federal government to turn its land to states, where private use of the public's resources is easier to achieve. Failing that, its strategy is to privatize all possible jobs working on federal lands, and to maximize commercial use.[60]

The Right also loathes government services that utilize public employees—another type of "socialism." Over time their lobbying has succeeded in privatizing many formerly government jobs—from the national parks to the War in Iraq.[61]

In terms of public land ownership combined with public sector employees, the American military is by far our largest "socialist" institution. Members of our armed forces do not work for private profit, but rather to serve the public good. There are no "entrepreneurs," no stock options. But the extreme Right won't criticize this major element of American "socialism." They don't want to seem unpatriotic.

The land and buildings of our public schools and universities are also "socialist," as are our schoolteachers and professors. (I suppose even our public university football teams are socialist.) Precisely because our education system is public it is a target for the extreme Right. Behind proposals to use tax funds and credits to fund private schools lies the "private is good; public is bad" philosophy.

Let's stop for a moment: Imagine that we were trying to establish our nationwide public school system today. Without question, the reactionary Right would be screaming that it was a socialist plot to take over America.

And how about the "socialist" Obama Administration?

Let's look at health care reform, Obama's flagship legislative effort. Far Right pundits and politicians shout that it's "socialism" and "a government takeover." Congressman Steve King of Iowa said on the floor of the House that the president was "shoving socialized medicine down the throats of the American people."

Socialized medicine is actually easy to define—it is the system used in almost all developed nations. Its defining element is insurance for all citizens, paid for by taxes and administered by the government.[62] Since there is no need for commercial advertising, high executive salaries, or hundreds of different health care plans, administrative costs in socialized insurance are much lower than for our privatized system. In some countries with socialized medicine, all medical staff are government employees; in others they are private sector; and in still others, they are a mixture of both. In all of these countries, the price of pharmaceutical drugs is controlled by the government, another major cost savings.

In the United States, we do have one fully socialized medical system. It is used to care for veterans of our armed forces. Veterans have taxpayer-funded insurance; Veteran Affairs (VA) doctors work on salary, not fee for service; and the VA sets the prices it will pay for drugs. (On average, the VA pays roughly 30 percent less for the same drugs as does Medicare, which is forbidden by Congress from negotiating drug prices.) Interestingly, these facts are not publicized by Fox News, and here again, the far Right does not attack veterans' socialist health care.

And how "socialist" is Obama's health care reform?

Progressives and liberals, plus many moderates and traditional conservatives, wanted three key elements in health care reform:

- Government-funded "single payer" insurance;

- Failing that, a "public option"—giving Americans a choice between a government-operated plan and private insurance;

- Government-regulated prices for pharmaceutical drugs.

The health care legislation passed by Congress and signed into law by President Obama contained none of these things. Our "reformed" health care system retains:

- Private, for-profit health insurance;

- Private doctors and medical staff;

- Private hospitals; and

- Private sector-set drug prices.

Directly put, it is a lie to call this "socialized medicine." So why does the extreme Right do it? Why do they lie? Because polling tells them that the American people do not like "socialism," and that by trumpeting the "socialist threat" they can accomplish three goals:

First, they can generate support for their political agenda to discredit the ability of our democratic government to solve our problems, thus limiting potential solutions to the private sector.

Second, they can divert attention from the disastrous economic failures of their privatization and deregulation ideology.

Third, they can prevent the American people from focusing on the central economic and political question of our time, which involves capitalism, not socialism.

And that question, which the Right is terrified that the American people will ask, is this: Can the global capitalist system be reformed so that it produces wealth not only for those at the top of the economic pyramid, but for *all* people—providing quality education for our children, health care for us all, decent wages and working conditions, and reliable pensions for the elderly? To achieve that, what changes need to be made?

As Americans, we can discuss and answer such basic questions if we are informed, engaged citizens—as the Founders intended. But we can only be informed, engaged citizens if the information we obtain is diverse, substantive, adequate, and truthful. Since polls show that most Americans rely on television as their main source of news, the erosion of in-depth, balanced, and factual broadcast news, current events, and educational programming threatens a cornerstone of our democracy.[63]

One can argue that if we want serious information, we can find it. And we can. But that does not answer the underlying question: If lax regulation combined with maximizing profits from the use of publicly owned airwaves hinders us from getting the information we need, should the American people do something about it?

And if another impact of profit-maximizing TV is the degradation of our children's moral values, should we intervene?

Many adults enjoy watching sexual programming, from suggestive to explicit pornography. Others like watching repetitive, bloody, explosive violence. As a result, sex and violence permeate TV. We can say, "That's all right. It's a personal, adult choice."

The trouble is, kids watch this stuff, too. And what they see on mainstream, prime-time TV is mind-numbing, astonishing violence and trashy, demeaning, soft-porn sex.

How much violence? An average child sees 8,000 murders on TV before leaving elementary school, and 200,000 violent acts by age eighteen.[64]

The sex on TV is not about healthy sexuality, love, and commitment. It is overwhelmingly sleazy, salacious, and degraded. A week or so before I wrote these lines I was watching TV on a Sunday afternoon. Flipping stations, I came to a program on TBS, a movie about teenagers. I watched as busty, bikini-clad girls rubbed each other's stomachs with body oil, moaning seductively. Then the male hero pulled a prank on his rival: He had the girls give the villain a jar of "cream" for his face. After the boy eagerly rubbed it over his cheeks and lips, and tasted it, he was told it was "stiffy juice"—semen.

Is this good for our kids? Does it help orient them for more fulfilling relationships, happier and more responsible lives? If not, do we need to accept it?

When I was growing up, no parent would have taken their child to see a movie containing what is now on television every day. Were they wrong then? And if not, what does that mean for what we are allowing to be put in front of our children now?

One hears the argument that it's the "parents' responsibility," meaning that each parent must *by themselves* challenge the seductive, immense power of commercial television. If for any reason they do not, or cannot, successfully do that, the argument goes, "That's their problem." In fact, it is *our* problem.

American children and adolescents today will have spent more time watching television than they have in the classroom when they graduate from high school.[65] This is unprecedented in human history. What is on TV matters for how each young person comes to define himself or herself—as an individual and as a citizen.

A close friend of mine was formerly head of a major movie studio and a top cable TV executive. He is an honorable man, highly respected for his talent and integrity. I sent him a recording of the "American Values for Our Time" speech that provided the basis for this book. He called me on the phone.

"Why are you giving that talk?" he asked. "Why all this focus on the media and television?"

I said I was speaking out because I believed it was necessary, and that as a country we needed to confront the issue. In the silence that followed, I realized my friend was not happy with what I was doing.

"Bill," I said, "I know how deeply you love your grandchildren. Do you believe that what is on TV is good for them?"

There was a long pause. Then he said, "No, I don't. All of us in the business know it's shit, but we don't know what the hell to do about it."

That comment reflects the human tragedy that we all face: Honorable people are trapped in a system of our own making.

Why do we allow gratuitous violence and sleazy sex on

prime-time, kids-accessible television shows? Because the dynamics of the industry demand conscienceless competition for market share and the advertising revenues that flow from it. And the people's government, charged under law with regulating the industry, does not do its job. In the absence of organized public outrage, nothing will change. TV will continue to damage our kids and our nation.

So will video games.

In 2005, 60 Minutes devoted a segment to Grand Theft Auto, one of the hottest-selling games. To play you simply select a car that you want to drive. There is a catch: The car is owned by someone else. With a gun or knife, you force them out of the car, and drive away. Then the police start chasing you. And you start killing them.

The killing is graphic. You cut off their heads and see the blood spurt. You blow them away and blood splatters everywhere. This continues until you kill all the police or they kill you.

60 Minutes told the story of a seventeen-year-old kid who had spent thousands of hours playing Grand Theft Auto over a period of two years. Then one day he hijacked a car—a real one. He was chased down by the police, arrested, and taken to the station. While they were booking him, he grabbed the arresting officer's gun and shot and killed him. A second officer came running and the boy killed him. He turned to leave, walked down a hall, saw a radio dispatcher, and killed him, too. He shot them all in the head, just like in the video game.

60 Minutes interviewed the game's distributor. "We are not in any way responsible for that," he said. "Most kids do not react that way."

It is the same answer TV executives give about the impact

on children of television sex and violence. It is the same answer given by sugar cereal merchants and tobacco companies: We are not responsible. There is no proven harm. It's the parents' responsibility.

What makes otherwise normal, decent human beings say things like this? What makes them deny obvious truths, violate basic human values?

Money.

Sex and violence aimed at kids generate hundreds of millions of dollars in profits. For those high enough up the ladder, benefits include first class air travel anywhere in the world, top-line hotels with deferential doormen, the best in restaurants, and vacations at exclusive resorts. Virtually anything you want in the world of material and physical pleasure. And in a society that has come to value wealth above all, social prestige and the envy of others. We are human. We are often willing to do what we know in our hearts is wrong if the temptation is big enough.

Should we do something about all this? Or is the matter outside the appropriate role of democratic government? What should be the test?

One hundred years ago, Theodore Roosevelt spoke to the people of the United States. He felt that huge fortunes were being made in ways that concentrated wealth in too few hands, that workers were not being paid adequate wages to support their families and give them a chance to move up the economic ladder. He believed this undermined the dynamism of the economy and the nation. This is what he said:

> We grudge no man a fortune in civil life if it is
> honorably obtained and well used. It is not even

enough that it should be gained without doing damage to the community. We should permit it to be gained only so long as the gaining represents benefit to the community.[66]

TAKING BACK TV

Properly used, TV can play a central role in helping us revitalize the Founders' values of personal and civic responsibility. To regain some balance and decency in TV we can start by insisting that more of its content serves, rather than undermines, our nation. And we have effective tools to make this happen.

As discussed earlier, the Federal Communications Commission issues licenses to broadcasters that enable them to generate hundreds of millions in profits. The FCC has authority to regulate program content and require broadcasters to take actions that serve the public good. Let's start with this. In the same way we charge a royalty fee for for-profit companies to mine minerals from public lands, we need to tax national TV ads that use the public airwaves as follows:

• Require national broadcasters to pay a fee based on advertising revenues. Use the proceeds to establish the American Values Advertising Fund, which will sponsor programs and public service ads that promote community, civic, and responsible personal and family values.

• Expand public broadcasting to include an array of world-class TV channels specifically for kids, teens, parents, and seniors, including top-quality educational shows and local news programs.[67] (In the United States we currently spend $1.31

per person on public media. Canadians spend $22 per capita, and the British $80.)

- Produce terrific public service ads to counter runaway consumerism, just as we now have anti-smoking ads. Let's have TV spots that promote responsible parenting, a strong work ethic, good citizenship, a sense of community, human compassion, generosity, honesty, personal responsibility: Show seniors mentoring kids in elementary school, a child being taught to play the piano; a family engaged in conversation over dinner; a parent reading a book to a child, kids exploring nature in the woods, a carpenter feeling good after finishing a hard day's work, a teenager volunteering in a nursing home or helping someone cross the street. Such ads will help us rediscover a living sense of community, the traditional American value of good-neighborliness, and the importance of citizenship.

Additionally, public service ads can help us focus on major national problems. For example, the rising obesity rates have tremendous human and economic costs. Innovative ads, sponsored by doctors' organizations, have been driving home the seriousness of the condition and effective strategies to overcome it. We need more ads like this on drug use, smoking, teenage drinking, and unwanted pregnancy—even ads to encourage people to turn off the TV!

Local and state governments and nonprofits would apply to the American Values Fund to finance the public service ads and local programming, and we can hold national competitions to judge the very best. The finest minds in advertising, now exploiting human frailties, would have the chance to use their talents to create ads that *help* people, that strengthen our sense of personal responsibility, caring, and common purpose. The potential of public interest advertising is immense. The same is true for locally and regionally produced programs. All that is lacking is the will and the funds to do it.

- A 5 percent tax would generate $7.5 billion a year, more than 17 times the present budget for the Corporation for Public Broadcasting—enough to fund new educational channels, hundreds of world-class programs, and sustained pro-people, pro-family, pro-community advertising.

- The FCC will need to re-establish serious public service requirements as a condition of broadcast licensing, including the airing of American Values ads.

- Additionally, Congress needs to extend the FCC's content-regulating authority to cable networks. Cable uses the public airwaves to distribute its programming—the legal basis for regulation—and it needs to function under the same rules as do traditional broadcast networks. Both broadcast and general access cable television programming featuring salacious sex and gratuitous violence needs to be banned from prime-time. A special tax should be levied on such programs and used to fund teen-oriented programming about healthy relationships and non-violent approaches to resolving conflict.

Critics will charge that these modest reforms amount to censorship and interference with private enterprise. The answer is yes on both counts: The American people have the right to insist that pursuing business profits does *not* include the right to harm the community, to harm our children. The Preamble to the Constitution charges the people's government with "promoting the general Welfare." It gives us the right and responsibility to insure that private enterprise is carried out responsibly, in ways that benefit the community.

Critics may also say it is not the business of government to use taxes to promote civic values. John Adams, Founder and second American president, disagreed. In 1779, while the Revolutionary War raged, he personally wrote the constitution for the Commonwealth of Massachusetts, the oldest functioning written constitution in the world. It contains this provision:

> Wisdom and knowledge, as well as virtue, diffused generally among the body of the people being necessary for the preservation of their rights and liberties; and as these depend on spreading the opportunities and advantages of education in various parts of the country, and among different orders of the people, it shall be the duty of legislators and magistrates in all future periods of this commonwealth to cherish the interests of literature and the sciences, and all seminaries of them, especially the university at Cambridge, public schools and grammar schools in the towns; to encourage private societies and public institutions . . . for the promotion of agriculture, arts, sciences, commerce, trade, manufactures, and a natural history of the country; to countenance and inculcate the principles of humanity and general

benevolence, public and private charity, industry and frugality, honesty and punctuality in their dealings, sincerity, good humor, and all social affections, and generous sentiments among the people.

The American Values Fund and reforms in TV content will not end the dominant role of commerce on the public airwaves. But they will be a significant step toward establishing balance by controlling program content that damages our kids, and by using the immense power of television not simply to sell products and make money, but to remind us and our children that, first and foremost, we are honorable people, family members, citizens, and a vital part of the American community.

CHAPTER 5

REVITALIZING CITIZENSHIP

Without hope we live in desire.
—DANTE ALIGHIERI, *The Inferno*, 1314

We need to do a better job of teaching good, old-fashioned patriotism—just that sense of loyalty and obligation to the community that is necessary for the preservation of all the privileges and rights that the community guarantees.
—GENERAL DWIGHT D. EISENHOWER, 1943

The majority of the Founders believed that everyday Americans would accept the rights and responsibilities of citizenship. But Alexander Hamilton did not. He argued that artisans, farmers, and laborers—everyday people—would never become sufficiently educated and informed to be trusted to control the government: "All communities divide themselves into the few and the many. The first are rich and wellborn, the other the mass of the people. . . . The people are turbulent and changing; they seldom judge or determine right. Give therefore the first class a distinct, permanent share in the government. They will check the unsteadiness of the second, as they cannot receive any advantage by a change, they therefore will ever maintain good government."[68]

But Jefferson, Madison, Washington, and the others were

convinced that every human being was born with an innate moral compass. All that was lacking was education—both formal education and the education of living in a democratic society freed from dictatorial power of propertied aristocrats, "divinely appointed" kings, and corrupted churches. They felt that, freed from economic, political, and religious oppression, everyday people would achieve their full potential as citizens and as human beings.

Two hundred fifty years later, it is fair to ask how well we are meeting their expectations.

Let's take voting, the foundational tool by which people control their government: George Washington and his troops endured the terrible winter at Valley Forge to achieve that elemental right for us. They lived in hovels and wore tattered rags against the bitter cold. Many had no shoes, food was scarce to nonexistent, and many men died. These American soldiers risked everything, gave all they had, to give to future generations the simple yet profound right to freely elect candidates to public office.

Yet today roughly one-third of our fellow countrymen do not consider it worth their time to register to vote. Many others register, but do not actually go to the polls. We consider it a great success when 60 percent of registered voters cast ballots for president—which means that a *minority* of eligible voters are deciding our national elections.[69] The average municipal election in the United States generates a pathetic 12 percent voter turnout. And a great many of us are stunningly uninformed. A 2010 Pew Research Center poll found that 18 percent of Republicans, 29 percent of Democrats, and 32 percent of independents did not know that Democrats controlled a majority in the House of Representatives. Fifty-one percent of young adults who were polled did not know Joe Biden was vice president![70] The Founders would be appalled. How can this be?

For most of our history a majority of Americans were rural, and our philosophy toward government was pretty well summarized by, "Leave me alone until I need something. When I do, I'll let you know." Until the twentieth century, the dynamism of the American nation did not seem to depend on the visible involvement of democratic government.[71] As a result, we have a longstanding political culture that stresses the "freedom" half of the American political equation, and places far less emphasis on the "civic responsibility" side.

FREEDOM AND COMMUNITY

In 2006 I spent fifty days driving across America as co-host of a documentary series about the state of the nation. We interviewed people from all walks of life, from homeless people to former Supreme Court Justice Sandra Day O'Connor. Among the questions we asked was, "What does it mean to you to be an American?" About 90 percent said, "Freedom." The freedom to "do what I want," "go where I want," "do the kind of work I want." Only one person said, "Freedom and the responsibility that goes along with it." Not a single person said, "The freedom to live in a democracy, the freedom to vote."

When America was largely a nation of farms and small towns, the "human scale" of town and business reinforced a natural sense of community, the realization of interdependence that in turn generates a sense of responsibility to each other. I grew up in Glen Ellen, California, a town of perhaps five hundred people. My first job was as a box boy and checker at the Valley of the Moon Market. I knew about 80 percent of the people who came into that grocery store, and they knew me; they knew the owners, Jack and Naomi Cate. I didn't understand it then, but what happened in the store was only partly commercial. It was also social. People came in to talk about the illness of a neighbor, the weather, fishing, the ball game. The simple fact that we knew each other and took time to talk reinforced our sense that we were part of a human community, that we were in this together.

When I was in college I worked in a gas station. I knew none of the customers, and I did not feel part of the community. Instead, it seemed there were simply a lot of people around, people to whom I had no connection.

A community's sense of equality and concern for each other is fundamental to democracy. But in today's fast-paced, commercial, urban America, *daily life generates a different sense of things*. We no longer see the neighbor family planting the wheat from which our mother makes bread, the blacksmith forging the shoes for our horse, the logger bringing in the timber to the sawmill that provides the lumber for the houses in town. We don't see Grandpa getting old in our own living room. We don't see the whole community turning out and working weekends for six months to build the new firehouse. We don't know the grocery store clerk. So long as we have credit cards and box stores, we can buy anything we want from anywhere in the world. But we don't know who made it, what wages they were paid, how they live, or if they need help.

Since democratic government is the tool we have for

making community decisions, why should we take democracy seriously if the "community" is invisible to us? Low voter turnout reflects many Americans' perception that voting, politics, and self-government are not relevant to their lives, and that personal freedom and civic engagement are not part of the same package.

The impact is profound: Those of us who fail to keep informed and fail to vote are breaking trust with the Founders. We are accepting the material benefits and personal freedoms of our American heritage, but not the responsibility that goes with the bargain. We are taking without giving, unintentionally undermining our democracy, our Constitution, and our nation.

The good news is, there are practical, cost-effective ways to change this situation, to help us actively embrace the rights *and* responsibilities of citizenship.

PUBLIC SCHOOLS

Let's start with "re-engineering" our public schools.

When I grew up, I had no idea the whole community was paying for my education—for the land and buildings, the teachers, the books, the buses. I did not know that one of the greatest achievements of the American people was the establishment of mandatory public education for all children. That single action opened opportunity to *all* people—across the historic barrier of economic class. It was a key reason the United States was able to build the strongest economy in the world.

Universal public education is paid for by every reader of this book, every adult American. All American children should know that, and learn to appreciate the gift.

To accomplish this, let's have every child, every semester, in every public school, write a note to someone picked at random from the telephone book:

> Dear Mrs. Harrison, I am Jane Johnson. I am in the second grade. I like math and art. I would like to be a scientist when I grow up. Thank you for helping to pay for my education.

That simple act, repeated twice a year throughout her schooling, would help every child understand an essential truth about being an American: your countrymen are supporting you. And every adult who receives such a letter would be touched in a tangible way by the truth that he or she is helping to educate a real, living child, and, by doing so, improving our nation. Getting letters from our nation's children would remind each of us that we are in fact contributing to our community, and enable us to say, "I feel *good* about that!"

We also need to modify what we teach in our schools. Many of us have come to think of education as the teaching of job-related skills. Yes, the twenty-first–century job market demands increased knowledge and skills, and education can provide it. But if all we expect our schools to do is to enable graduates to get well-paying jobs in a consumer economy, we fall into a trap of our own making.

In 2003 I interviewed Paul Trout, English professor at Montana State University. He described how "market values" had permeated higher education: University administrations routinely refer to students as "customers" for whom the college is providing "a product." Since higher education is expensive, and colleges are in intense competition for enrollments, parents and prospective students are told that their "investment" in higher education will pay off in enhanced earning power.

According to Trout, many students now believe that the hefty tuition they pay *entitles* them to "A" grades. What else are they paying for? And if they do not get the "A," it is the professor, not the student, who is to blame. Faculty at MSU receive "grades" from students, and those grades affect teacher salaries. In Trout's view, the combined effect of all this is a dumbing down of grading, reduction of student effort, lower academic performance, and a fundamental perversion of the educational process.

A January 2007 Pew Foundation poll found that 81 percent of American young people believe that the top priority of their generation is to "get rich." With that mindset, education becomes only a means to a materialistic end.[72]

The Founders saw it differently. To them, education would provide Americans with the knowledge, philosophical depth, and discerning judgment to be *informed citizens*, the bedrock of democracy.

In part because of excessive emphasis on teaching job-related skills, many of our young people remain ignorant of essential knowledge: In a recent survey of top liberal arts colleges, more than 50 percent of seniors believed that Germany, Japan, or Italy was an ally of the United States in World War II.[73] In another survey, students were asked to identify these words from the Declaration of Independence: ". . . that to secure these rights, governments are instituted among men, deriving their just powers from the consent of the governed; that whenever any form of government becomes destructive of these ends, it is the right of the people to alter or abolish it. . . ." Many said it was Karl Marx.[74]

When I interviewed former Supreme Court Justice Sandra Day O'Connor in 2006, I asked if she thought the American people in general understood the role of an independent judiciary. She said no, and added that many in Congress did not either. O'Connor said that in her time, school children seriously studied the Constitution, but not anymore. She said she was participating in a national effort to make it part of every student's curriculum.

The fact is that most of our children do not understand the foundations of the American nation. They need to. So, as we teach them to read and write, and to think critically, let's have them read and discuss Jefferson, Madison, Adams, Hamilton, and Lincoln. Let's be certain they learn America's founding values, understand the origin and meaning of the Declaration of Independence, and the provisions of the Constitution and Bill of Rights. They need to know the centrality to our democracy of the separate branches of government, the vital role of dissent and a free press, how Americans have used those tools to improve our country, and their own personal responsibility as citizens to their community and their nation:

- *In order to graduate from high school, every student should be required to pass a comprehensive test on founding values, the Constitution, and the responsibilities of citizenship.*

Further, citizenship should not only be taught in class. Students should experience it first-hand, as well. There are a hundred ways to enable this. In Helena, Montana, where I live, the local school district cooperates with the US Forest Service in the Youth Forest Monitoring Program, a seven-week summer internship where students get out on the ground and do real work. They monitor water quality in local creeks, evaluate vegetation, and collect data that the Forest Service uses to make ongoing management decisions impacting our public lands. The students get hands-on experience and the satisfaction of seeing their work have an impact in the real world. I attended an awards ceremony for the kids and their parents. The pride and enthusiasm they felt was clear.

The Montana Heritage Project, a multi-year effort funded by the Liz Claiborne/Art Ortenberg Foundation, also involved school kids directly with their communities. Students did their own research projects, digging into the history of their town, and interviewing elders in the community. They learned about World War II from *someone who was there*; they learned what their town was like before they were born. I've interviewed teachers and kids involved in this program, and it was clear what a powerful experience it was for them.

Instead of sitting at home playing video games, we need to get our kids out in the community, experiencing the connections that modern technology hides.

UNIVERSAL SERVICE

These steps alone will not overcome the constant "you are first and foremost a consumer" propaganda that bombards our children throughout their lives. So let's offer *every* young American an experience that brings to life the truth that they are responsible and valued members of the American community:

- *When leaving high school, every young American should provide the nation with one year of public service. The work could be civilian or military, and would include an array of choices: Planting trees and restoring stream banks in our national forests; tutoring elementary school kids; providing care in an elder care facility; serving in the United States military; working for the Red Cross, as a Peace Corps member abroad, or AmeriCorps Vista volunteer here at home.*

Every American youth would contribute this year of service as a way of thanking the community and the nation that provided his or her public education—a tremendous gift, essential to the youth's success in life. The work would provide young Americans with a sense of pride, knowing they were doing something important, for others and for their country. In return, the nation would know that *every young American* was acknowledging their debt, and deserved respect and honor for providing important service to the nation. Each person who serves could receive a basic wage, plus either a savings bonus or college tuition credits.

Universal service will reflect the living reality of mutual commitment and responsibility: We are American citizens, in this together.

It is a lesson we all need to relearn. Example: About 50 million Americans rely on Social Security to make ends meet.[75] Today's recipients paid into the system over many years and believe they are getting back what they put in. But for the large majority, that is not true. Because of inflation and the fact that people are living much longer than their parents, the contributions most people made are not enough to pay their current benefits. As a result, today's wage earners and their employers together pay an amount equal to 12.4 percent of the employees' gross pay to help fund the benefits of today's retirees.[76] Without that contribution, $660 billion a year, the system would collapse.

Social Security is the largest ongoing transfer of wealth from one generation to another in American history. Yet many of the beneficiaries don't know it! And since they believe they "earned it," they do not appreciate the sacrifice the younger generation is making on their behalf. Seniors vote in higher numbers than any other age group. If they feel no sense of interdependence with younger generations, they are more likely to vote against the local school bond, funds for education, or other social programs. But if our seniors understand that their Social Security check depends on the next generation of Americans getting a good education—and good jobs—they will bring a different perspective to the voting booth.

To help remind today's retirees about the realities of Social Security:

▪ Every envelope containing a Social Security check should contain a photograph of a working man or woman or business owner who is paying Social Security taxes, a short description of that person's family, and the work they do, plus a summary of why their contribution is essential to the viability of Social Security: a monthly reminder that we are in this together.

In a key respect, citizenship is alive and well in America. We are the most philanthropic nation in the world. People from all economic classes give generously to a wide array of social and environmental causes. By definition, philanthropy means that the donor sees beyond "me" to "we," and identifies strongly with the welfare of the whole. The word itself derives from the Greek *philos*, loving, and *anthropos*, man.

In 2006 I visited St. Jude Children's Hospital in Memphis, Tennessee. It is one of the world's preeminent care and research centers, treating four thousand children a year for cancer and other catastrophic diseases. Unlike businesses that patent medical discoveries for profit, St. Jude shares all research findings worldwide. Treatment is given at no charge to the patient.

I was stunned to learn that roughly *6 million* individual Americans regularly contribute to the hospital, with an average donation of $25.68. In 2005, including all sources of funds, they had raised almost $600 million, 10 percent more than St. Jude's annual budget.

Perhaps the most important advantage of charitable giving over government-funded social services is that, in making the choice to give, the donor feels a sense of personal connection that is lacking when his or her tax dollars, pooled with millions of other peoples' tax dollars, are used to help people in need.

That fact does not alter the need for major public expenditures to meet human needs. But tax-funded services should learn from philanthropy, and seek ways to reinforce the feeling of personal involvement of the taxpayer with the fate and welfare of others, as proposed by the simple suggestions made above.

The same sense of community is reflected in our nation's tremendous tradition of volunteerism, unsurpassed in the world. From 2007 to 2009, an average of 62 million Americans gave of their time to volunteer for social causes, based on their religious, spiritual, or secular commitment to the human community. They donated an average of more than thirty-four hours per person—a total of 8 billion hours.[77]

Like those who give financially, people who donate time to civic needs share a living commitment to the welfare of our human community. Despite the new technology and material affluence that surrounds us, we remain the same special creatures we have been from our beginning—human beings. We are simultaneously separate individuals, thinking and acting alone, and social beings, dependent on the larger community for the essentials of life. Deep inside, we yearn for more than an exclusively self-focused life—a truth reflected in a recent poll conducted of freshman entering religious colleges. Despite having been raised in our consumer culture, 75 percent said that it was important to them to be part of something bigger than themselves. Our great nation has the ability, and the responsibility, to offer all of our young people—and all of us—the chance to experience that deeper meaning.

CHAPTER 6

CHECKS AND BALANCES

Exactly as the special interests of cotton and slavery threat-
ened our political integrity before the Civil War, so now the
great special business interests too often control and corrupt
the men and methods of government for their own profit.
We must drive the special interests out of politics.

—THEODORE ROOSEVELT, 1910

The liberty of a democracy is not safe if the people tolerate
the growth of private power to a point where it becomes
stronger than the democratic state itself.

—PRESIDENT FRANKLIN ROOSEVELT, 1938

If a visitor should come to this country from another planet,
would he not find it strange that in this country so much
power is permitted to private corporations without their
having commensurate responsibility?

—ALBERT EINSTEIN, 1945

The Founders were very careful in establishing the structure
of the new American government. They had studied history and knew the tragic consequences of concentrated
power. And they understood the contradictory truth that we
humans are, on the one hand, creative, noble, loving, and gen-

erous, and, on the other, suspicious, violent, fearful, and greedy. They understood that all human institutions are subject to human flaws, and went to great lengths in the Constitution and Bill of Rights to establish a system of checks and balances. Their goal was to limit and decentralize governmental power enough to avoid dictatorship, repression, and the denial of central human rights.

One hundred years later Theodore Roosevelt realized that the same concept was necessary for the economy. A dynamic personality, he served as governor of New York, vice president of the United States, and president, and was a member of the Progressive wing of the Republican Party.[78] A competitive personality, T. R. believed in the competition generated by genuinely free markets. But he understood that the essential nature of big business, with its relentless pursuit of increased profits and market share, led to huge enterprises that used their power to stifle competition, monopolize the marketplace, and undermine equality of economic opportunity for everyday people. And he understood that to protect their commercial position they would attempt to control our government.

T. R. understood that concentrated *private* power was as dangerous as concentrated public power. As president, he used anti-trust legislation passed by his Progressive allies to fight monopolies. Market competition was impractical with railroads, which gouged customers on shipping freight. So T. R. pushed Congress to create the Interstate Commerce Commission, with authority to set maximum rates. In response to health scandals in the meatpacking industry, he pressed for establishment of the Pure Food and Drug and Meat Inspection acts, laying the groundwork for modern consumer protection. He and his friend and political ally Gifford Pinchot established federal agencies to protect federally owned natural resources from outright, rampant theft, and to manage them for the long-term benefit of the people. He did these things to establish checks on the abuse by private power of the public interest.

T. R.'s efforts were vehemently opposed by people who believed that private economic interests (their own) should have priority over those of the public. They opposed his attempts to control monopolies and regulate railroads; they opposed his efforts to end graft and the private theft of natural resources from public lands. Forerunners of today's free market "conservatives," they were extremely powerful within Roosevelt's own party and fought effectively against him. The fight split the Republican Party, and in the end, T. R.'s Progressives lost and the privatizers won. Their "private over public" ideology still controls the Republican Party, and over time has also come to wield great influence in the Democratic Party, as well.

Bill Clinton played a key role in that shift, leading a Democratic faction that called itself centrist, and supported "free trade" on corporate terms. Like Britain's Tony Blair, Clinton argued that corporate-friendly policies would bring strong growth to the economy, and new revenues for education, health care, and combating poverty. As president, Clinton fought for the passage of the North American Free Trade Agreement (NAFTA), corporate-written rules governing trade between Canada, the United States, and Mexico. The political battle divided Democrats, with liberals, progressives, and trade unions in opposition. A majority of congressional Democrats voted against NAFTA, but with Republican support, Clinton got it passed.

Clinton's thinking was influenced by a simple political equation: Election campaigns had become extremely expensive, and Republicans often raised twice the money of Democrats. Money is power, and the powerful have money. They gave generously to support Republican policies to reduce taxes on corporations, high incomes, and capital gains, to increase private sector profits by privatizing government services and deregulating business. Clinton's "centrists" were determined to tap into that money stream. All they needed to do was to adopt pro-corporate strategies, and they did.

The results were not long in coming. In 1992 Democratic National Committee (DNC) soft money contributions from business interests were $12,214,420, only two-thirds the Republicans' take. In 1994, they jumped to $19 million, equaling the Republicans. Two years later, the parties raked in $47 million each.[79] The Clinton-era chair of the DNC, Ron Brown, was famous for his corporate fundraising, and frank about the new Democratic approach to "advancing strategic business interests."[80]

Today, both major American political parties are dependent on business and corporate financing. As a result, those interests almost always determine economic policy. So American workers are competing against Chinese workers who receive sixty cents an hour for a ten-hour day. From the profit-maximizing perspective of a global corporation, this disparity is a terrific opportunity for enhanced profit and increased share value. It looks different to American wage earners.

After the Depression-era formation of large trade unions, rough checks and balances developed within the American economic structure: Business interests were balanced by the power of millions of organized union members able to bargain over wages and working conditions, and if necessary, to go on strike: Ford Motor Company's factories were in Detroit, which meant that organized workers there had power. In the 1953, union members comprised 36 percent of the American workforce, and used that power to push for higher pay, health benefits, and pensions.[81] During those decades real income of the entire working middle class rose dramatically.

But under globalized "free trade" rules, Ford can have parts and cars made anywhere, and labor's ability to provide a "check and balance" is vastly reduced. The result? American median wages have stagnated, union membership has plummeted to 7 percent of the private workforce, and tens of millions of manufacturing jobs have shifted to developing nations. China is now the second largest economy overall, and is predicted to emerge as the world's largest manufacturer within a decade.[82]

Some argue that Chinese wages will rise over time, enhancing their standard of living and creating a level playing field with American workers. But supply and demand suggest a different picture: *the number of unemployed and underemployed in China alone is larger than the entire US workforce, and the number of honor students in Chinese schools exceeds the total number of students in America. In China and the rest of the developing world, hundreds of millions of desperate people are standing in line for poverty-level jobs, assuring long-term downward pressure on wages.*[83] As Chinese workers demand higher pay, there is an infinite supply of workers elsewhere around the globe who will accept even lower wages. This vicious cycle hurts not just American workers and their families, but also those in impoverished countries.

Of course, this is all good news for global corporate profits. And the election money warp leads Congress and American presidents to support these corporate-centered globalization policies.

The same money warp affects domestic policy as well. Wal-Mart employs more than *two million* Americans. The company earned $14.4 billion in profits in 2009.[84] Yet an in-depth study in 2005 found that the company's wages were so low that "each new Wal-Mart worker is causing the average state to expend just under $900 in Medicaid benefits."[85] Medicaid is the publicly funded health insurance program for the poor. So Wal-Mart makes enormous profits, its workers receive poverty-level wages, and the American taxpayer picks up the health insurance tab. Additionally, the arrival of Wal-Mart in any town is assured to destroy many local, family-owned businesses and jobs. Our country needs a legitimate debate about such issues, and whether or not federal policy should require better wages and benefits from companies like Wal-Mart. But that debate is not genuine if the ultimate arbitrators—our elected representatives—have been pre-selected by the money warp to support corporate interests.

The Founders went to great pains to ensure checks and balances between branches of our government. But they did not anticipate the emergence of our extraordinarily expensive electoral process, or the control over our democracy that is exercised by the financial power of corporate interests.

Abraham Lincoln defined the fundamental condition of democracy: "Allow all the governed an equal voice in the government, and that, and that only, is self-government." Today's big money politics makes that impossible, subverting the essence of government "of the people, by the people and for the people." We can preserve our democracy, and re-establish checks and balances in our political system, by ending the lobbying and election money warp, strengthening workers' rights, and redefining the legal privileges and responsibilities of corporations.

ELIMINATING THE MONEY WARP

The goal of election finance reform must be to provide an effective counterbalance to special interest money. Yet in the stunning 2010 Supreme Court ruling *Citizens United v. Federal Election Commission*, the Court's "conservative" majority effectively struck down even the modest, congressionally established limits on corporate money in political campaigns. In a 5–4 vote, the Court ruled that corporations and unions, although not human beings, enjoyed the full First Amendment rights intended by the Founders for people. They also chose to ignore the simple truth that corporate entities command vast sums of money, which overwhelm the financial capacity of everyday citizens.

The Court majority should have reminded themselves of what Teddy Roosevelt had to say about the rights of corporations: "For every special interest is entitled to justice, but not one is entitled to a vote in Congress, to a voice on the bench, or to representation in any public office. The Constitution guarantees protection to property, and we must make that promise good. But it does not give the right of suffrage to any corporation. . . . There can be no effective control of corporations while their political activity remains."[86]

Until the Court's decision is reversed, or the Constitution amended, campaign reform law cannot prohibit special interest expenditures. But we can do something:

- Candidates for federal office can have a choice:
Accept large private contributions, or use a federally funded system of campaign financing. To qualify for the public system, candidates must agree to a $500 limit for individual contributions, and forego those from Political Action Committees, political groups, corporations, or unions. In return, they receive public funds that match the "over $500" individual and special interest contributions received by their opponent.

- All candidates receive free postage for campaign mailings and reduced-fee access to radio and television for campaign ads.[87]

- As a condition of their FCC license, broadcasters would be required to provide cut-rate advertising to candidates for federal office.

Such a system would fundamentally change the playing field, guaranteeing that candidates who decline large private contributions would be equally able to get their message to voters as those who rely on personal fortunes or special interest money. Since the new rules would eliminate the advantage of taking big private money, who would choose to seek or use it? True, someone of extreme wealth might still choose to spend some of their own money anyway, but they would have the strong disincentive of knowing they could not outspend their opponent. Not a perfect solution, but a fundamental improvement over the money warp we have now.

Overwhelmingly, most candidates would accept the no-PAC and $500 limitations. As a result, the public "match" of big special interest money would rarely be needed.[88]

REFORMING THE CORPORATE STRUCTURE

The laws I mentioned earlier, establishing an overarching "fiduciary duty" of corporate officers to maximize shareholder value, made sense in the eighteenth and nineteenth centuries. Communications were slow and unreliable, few regulations existed, and the ability to monitor corporate activity was weak. But as Theodore Roosevelt understood, an exclusive focus on profit-driven shareholder value, combined with the economic power of corporations, has far-reaching and negative impacts.

Henry Ford, auto magnate and mass production pioneer, learned that lesson in a very personal way. He believed that it made good business sense to pay his factory workers a high enough wage that they could buy Ford cars. In 1914, that meant five dollars a day instead of the three-dollar industry standard, as well as low pricing of his cars. The automaker said, "To our way of thinking, this was an act of social justice, and in the last analysis, we did it for our own satisfaction of mind. There is pleasure in feeling you have made others happy—that you have lessened in some degree the burdens of your fellow-men—that you have provided a margin out of which there may be had pleasure and saving."

Ford was criticized by the *Wall Street Journal* for injecting "Biblical or spiritual principles into a field where they do not belong." There has never been a more succinct summary of the corporate mindset.[89]

Two of Ford's major shareholders, John and Horace Dodge, were using Ford dividends to manufacture their own brand of cars. They brought suit against Ford, asserting that, by paying his workers more than the market required, he was reducing company profits and their stock dividends. In a landmark case, the Dodge brothers won. By paying his workers more than the minimum required, the court held, Ford was breaching his corporate duty.[90]

What would happen if corporate law was modified to require that major corporations, in addition to shareholder value, consider the impact of their actions on the well-being of their workers, the communities in which they operate, the environment, and the nation?

The *Wall Street Journal*'s arguments against Henry Ford were echoed seventy years later by Milton Friedman, leading "free market/libertarian" economist. He claimed that broadening the charter of corporations to include social considerations would pervert their essential purpose: to mobilize capital to generate wealth. In his view, the cumulative impact of thousands of major corporations pursuing narrow financial self interest inevitably leads to wealth creation that benefits everyone.

As we have seen, the facts prove otherwise. For the last thirty years, while the Gross Domestic Product tripled, worker productivity increased, and corporate profits and the stock market soared until the crash of 2008, income of middle-class Americans has been static, and lower-income people have lost 20 percent of their share of the national income. The gap between the super rich and everyone else is wider than ever and still growing.

Friedman and his disciples argue that pursuit of maximum profit requires constant efforts to minimize costs through increases in efficiency. They ignore the parallel truth that cost reduction is often achieved at the expense of employees and by pushing what should be corporate costs onto the public. So Wal-Mart's poverty-level wages result in taxpayers picking up the health care costs for the children of the corporation's workers.

EMPLOYEE RIGHTS

As mentioned earlier, in his first annual message to Congress in 1861, Abraham Lincoln wrote, "Labor is prior to, and independent of capital. Capital is only the fruit of labor, and could never have existed had labor not first existed. Labor is the superior of capital, and deserves much the higher consideration."

Yet for most of the 150 years since then, our government's laws and regulations have favored capital over labor. From the last half of the nineteenth century until the economic crash of 1929, American industry, banking, and the owners of private fortunes wielded immense power, in many cases controlling local, state, and even the federal government. This government-business alliance was best summed up by President Calvin Coolidge in 1925: "The chief business of the American people is business."[91] His view was shared by business leaders. When Herbert Hoover was nominated in 1928 to succeed Coolidge, the *Wall Street Journal* wrote, "Never before, here or anywhere else, has a Government been so completely fused with business. . . . Hoover would serve the public by serving business. . . ."[92]

A year later, the *laissez-faire* party ended with the crash of the stock market, the closing of thousands of banks, and the onset of the Great Depression.

Franklin Roosevelt was elected in 1932 and, in response to the worst economic crisis in our nation's history, imposed wide-ranging regulations on the stock market, finance, utilities, transportation, and many other industries. The experience of the Depression was so powerful that the need for government intervention in the economy was not really challenged until Ronald Reagan's election as president in 1980. In the three decades since, business deregulation, self-regulation, privatization of public services, and pro-business policies have become dominant, reflected in corporate-friendly rules of globalization. These realities have dramatically strengthened management's power over employees, enabling companies to threaten to move jobs overseas if workers push for better wages and working conditions. In the absence of union representation, individual workers have absolutely no bargaining power against such pressures. The resulting wage and benefit rollbacks ripple through the entire American work force. Yet trade union membership in the United States is at an all-time low, having declined from almost 40 percent of the workforce in the 1950s to 7 percent of private sector workers today. Declining union membership is in part a consequence of aggressive corporate anti-union tactics, including the firing of pro-union workers. Strong worker representation at the bargaining table not only improves wages and working conditions for those directly involved. It has a ripple effect throughout the economy, setting a standard that others must take into account. In the fifties, when union representation was strong, wages and income rose sharply for most Americans. But when only one in fifteen private workers is represented by a union, that critical leverage is lost. It will be impossible to reestablish balance between corporations and their employees without enhancing workers' ability to form trade unions. Additionally, we need to provide strong incentives for corporations to adopt the "co-determination" model commonly used in Europe, where up to 49 percent of corporate board membership and other management bodies are set aside for worker representation.[93] Ensuring workers have a strong voice at the corporate policy-making table would help to reestablish checks and balances in our economic system.

ENVIRONMENTAL COSTS

Corporate "values" are fully comfortable with forcing the taxpayer to pay for damage caused by business activity. The mining industry is a classic case of this "externalizing" of costs: In the nineteenth and twentieth centuries, mining corporations played a pivotal role in providing minerals for America's industrial infrastructure. In Montana, the Anaconda Mining and Smelter Company in 1916 employed more than 10,000 workers and produced 352 million pounds of copper. They also controlled most of the state's newspapers, the state legislature, and the governor's office. The processes used to extract and smelt the copper ore resulted in massive deforestation, and pollution of rivers and groundwater. The Berkeley Pit in Butte and eighty miles of the Clark Fork River became toxic. Hundreds of millions of dollars and penalties assessed against Anaconda's purchaser, ARCO, have been needed to partially correct the devastation.

In reaction to these sorts of disasters, Congress passed the Superfund law in 1980, which placed a tax on mining to pay for cleaning up past pollution. Congress and many states passed tougher anti-pollution laws to avoid future problems.

The response of mining companies was predictable: First, they worked to weaken or repeal the anti-pollution laws; next, they tried to eliminate the Superfund tax; and then they moved their mining operations to other nations with low wages and weak environmental laws. Every one of these actions was fully compatible with—even required by—market pressures and the legal responsibility of corporate officers to maximize shareholder value. Every one of these actions directly harmed people, the environment, and the health of our planet.

"EVERYBODY NEEDS A SPEED LIMIT"

In 2001, I interviewed a Montana mining engineer on my radio show. He was a sincere and intelligent man who criticized "environmentalists who drive around in cars made of metal, but oppose mining." He made the point that we all use the products of mines but seem to want the extraction done in someone else's back yard. He said that excessively tough environmental laws had resulted in the mining industry moving to poverty-stricken nations where workers were exploited and the environment damaged with impunity. He argued that, from a global perspective, mining elsewhere was causing far more harm than if it had been conducted using better practices in the United States.

I said that I thought he raised valid points. Then I asked him a question: "The mining industry assures the people of the United States that it has learned its lesson from the past, and can be trusted now to mine responsibly. So why is it that the same companies who make these claims conduct their overseas operations in a way that you yourself say pollutes the environment and exploits workers?"

He paused for a second, then said, "Everybody needs a speed limit."

Fair enough. Without "speed limits"—legal restraints on our behavior—many of us are tempted to take actions out of self-interest that will harm the larger community. That is precisely why we have laws. When democracy is working right, those laws reflect the checks and balances arising from diverse and competing private and public interests. It is an imperfect balance, ever changing. But it works.

The problem arises when some forces become so powerful that there are no adequate checks on them. Today, there is no public power strong enough to provide balance to corporate power. Banks lobbied successfully to eliminate regulations enacted during the New Deal, then are allowed to become "too big to fail," cause a financial collapse, then demand—and receive—hundreds of billions of taxpayer dollars so they can keep functioning.

Again, the issue is not about "bad people." It is about normal human beings working in a setting that over time erodes ethical values and often triggers irresponsible, harmful behavior. There are thousands of sharks swimming in the corporate sea, living and dying by the soulless laws of market survival. If a corporation tries to break the sharks' rules and take actions that benefit society but reduce profit, it will almost certainly be eaten.

In the 1990s I was director of the Montana Nature Conservancy and got to know Ted Turner well. I once asked him if he could reduce the amount of graphic violence on Turner Broadcasting programs. As a parent and grandparent, he agreed that such programming was harming our nation's children. He is also a billionaire who has given generously of his personal wealth to fight poverty, protect the environment, and prevent nuclear proliferation. In short, Turner is a man of influence and social conscience. He owned TBS, but he didn't hesitate for one second before answering: "No way. We do that and we lose market share. We'll get eaten alive."

So while Ted Turner uses millions to try to do good, the *multi-billion* dollar business that generates his personal wealth subverts his own moral values. It's a losing game.

Normal citizens accept both rights and responsibilities. We instinctively understand that we do not have the "right" to harm others. Democracy depends on those human qualities. But the corporate structure is not "human"; its rules of operation make irrelevant such fundamental values as generosity, compassion, hope, love, faith, and patriotism. These essential qualities that make us human are not "market values."

In the mid-1990s I was driving to Belt, Montana, with Republican governor Marc Racicot. Marc was raised Catholic in the small timber town of Libby, Montana, and was serious about his faith. As we drove we talked about economics and ethics, markets and morality. Finally he turned to me and said, "Remember, the market has no conscience."[94]

Power without conscience is dangerous. It damages our human community in exact relationship to the power it has. Today multilayered and multinational corporations wield immense power, often without the constraints of human values. To protect ourselves, to protect the lives and happiness of our children and grandchildren, we must change that. We need to reform corporate law to bring commerce in line with conscience, the making of money in accord with morality.

The fact is that many corporations have pursued enlightened employment practices and socially and environmentally conscious initiatives—Ford, Goodyear, Pfizer, Costco, Starbuck's, Patagonia, Orvis, and BP (yes, BP!), to name a few. And several years ago, one hundred CEOs from some of the world's largest corporations even signed an agreement to adhere to the principles of the Universal Declaration of Human Rights, which includes provisions for paying living wages. But the overriding legal duty of executives to shareholder value, combined with perpetual competition from companies that put corporate earnings above all, places essential limits on the breadth and scale of such efforts, and makes them the exception, rather than the rule. We need legal reform that makes them the rule, not the exception.

To do that, we need to create new federal law that re-affirms and revitalizes the purpose for which government used its power to create corporations in the first place: To further the public good.

In exchange for the special privileges corporations receive, the new law will:

▪ Require all publicly held corporations that engage in commerce in the United States to include in their charters or registry in the United States the responsibility to conduct business in a manner that furthers the welfare of their employees, the natural environment, the communities in which they operate, and the American nation; and to appoint an ombudsman with the authority and responsibility to monitor the corporations' fulfillment of its public interest responsibilities and to suggest ways of achieving them. The provisions of this requirement will need careful drafting to achieve two goals. First, to assure that a legal duty is created defining acceptable corporate behavior. Second, to clearly define the scope and limits of that duty so as enable shareholder actions to enforce it, while minimizing the potential of frivolous litigation;

▪ Establish that investing in social and environmental initiatives is an activity "beneficial to the corporation" under the law, even if it reduces shareholder value; and specifically protect corporate officers from shareholder challenge to such activities;

▪ Insure that all international trade agreements to which the United States is a party include enforceable provisions that require our trading partners and companies that sell products in our nation to 1) ban child labor; 2) guarantee workers the right to form independent trade unions with real protections against harassment and intimidation; and 3) enact and enforce modern environmental protections comparable to our own. These provisions will help level the playing field in global trade, enhance economic human rights and living conditions around the world, and help to reverse global damage to the environment. They will also reduce the advantage that multinational corporations gain by employing overseas workers instead of Americans.

We also need to:

▪ Create significant tax incentives to encourage formation of "co-determination" corporations on the European model, where workers have major representation corporate governing bodies; and

▪ Consult with corporate leaders and reform experts who have demonstrated their commitment to responsible corporate behavior, and consider additional measures to get the job done.

In combination, these steps can create a corporate presence in our world that continues to generate wealth and opportunity, but does so in ways that enhance the welfare of our human community, that brings commerce together with conscience.

These proposals will generate vehement opposition from interests that profit from the status quo. Like other proposals in this book, they will be criticized by free market "conservatives" and the extreme Right as "social engineering," the label used to attack efforts by the government to address environmental problems, racial discrimination, or concentrated economic power.

The criticism is not new. President Franklin Roosevelt was attacked for "social engineering" during the Great Depression when he put people to work with government-funded jobs, established Social Security, and pushed for legislation giving workers the right to organize unions; the same label was used against the United States Supreme Court when it banned racial segregation in public schools; Medicare was called "socialist social engineering."

Yet the label is never used against government policies that benefit corporations or the wealthy—the hundreds of tax loopholes, subsidies and special deals achieved by lobbyists. The Bush Administration's $700 billion Wall Street and bank bailout in 2008 was not criticized as "social engineering." Nor did the far Right make that charge when the 2001 and 2003 tax cuts were proposed and passed, largely benefiting the economic elite and generating an additional $2.3 trillion in national debt over ten years.[95]

The truth is that *any* attempt to use government policies to benefit any part of society is social engineering. Our Founders were the greatest of social engineers: They established the American democratic Republic. The Louisiana Purchase was massive social engineering, in Jefferson's words, "to expand the empire of Liberty." So was giving millions of acres of public land to homesteaders and railroad companies, the building of public highways to generate jobs and enhance transportation of goods; establishing and funding our public school system to enhance the education of our people; requiring competence tests to practice law or medicine as a way of assuring high-quality professional services; granting homeowners a tax deduction for mortgage interest to encourage home ownership; providing price supports for farmers; or giving tax breaks to oil companies to encourage exploration. Each of these policies and hundreds of others are designed to "engineer" some change in society. The question up for debate, then, is not whether something is or is not social engineering but only whether the impact will be good or bad, whether it is in line with our founding values, whether it is respectful of liberties and rights, and whether it is worth the cost.

WEALTH AND TAXES

As discussed earlier, the top 25 percent of Americans own about 87 percent of the private wealth; the top 1 percent own

34 percent.[96] Is such concentration of wealth good or bad for the economy? Is it good for America? The world?[97]

To consider the answers, we need to ask a more fundamental question: What is the *purpose* of the economy? I think most of us might answer something like this: "The basic purpose of the economy is to generate wealth that benefits those who participate in it, and the human community who the economy serves." In order to be able to pass on those benefits and wealth to future generations, the economy also needs to function in a way that preserves the life-sustaining elements of our planet, including clean water and air, fertile soil, and diverse plants and animals.

If we can broadly agree on those fundamentals, how does today's wealth concentration stack up?

Let's skip for the moment whether it meets any common sense test of fairness for one man (a George Soros, David Koch, Bill Gates, or any one the world's 500+ billionaires) to have as much personal wealth as the combined wealth of tens of millions of households in America.[98] Instead, let's look at the hard-nosed, practical side.

Many economists argue that reducing wealth and income inequality is good for the economy: The wealthy, they argue, spend a much lower portion of their income than average families; and they are able to invest the rest anywhere in the world where return looks promising. Many of those investments do not help the American economy. In contrast, middle-and low-income people spend nearly all the money they make—here in the USA. Increasing their income, by either raising wages or extending the Earned Income Tax Credit upward through the middle class, these economists argue, will spur demand and economic growth. Bottom-up economics instead of "trickle down."

And there is something more fundamental involved.

Every normal human being has the innate intelligence and ability to contribute to the economy by generating wealth and the benefits that flow from it. So, insuring that each person obtains the fundamental rearing, training, and knowledge to do so serves *everyone's* economic interest. Teddy Roosevelt was a fiercely competitive man, and a vocal advocate of disciplined competition in the economy. He said, "Equality of opportunity means that the commonwealth will get from every citizen the highest service of which he is capable."[99] In his view, since all benefited from the economic results arising from equal opportunity, we all needed to pay for the basic social infrastructure that made genuine opportunity possible.

In today's world, having equal opportunity for every citizen requires at least these fundamentals: adequate nutrition, shelter, and clothing; high-quality education; and access to affordable health care. Clearly, unregulated market forces do *not* assure those fundamentals to all working citizens and their families.

The social infrastructure that *creates* equal economic opportunity and the wealth it generates—such as quality schools, public transportation, and health care access—is in need of serious investment. Who should pay?

Obviously, we *all* should pay.[100] Honest, genuinely conservative common sense says that if you accept the benefit you need to be willing to pay your fair share of the cost.

So what is a "fair share"?

Adam Smith is regarded as a near god by free market "conservatives." They like to quote his opinion that the self-interested interaction of the small merchants of his time (the late 1700s) benefited the whole community with "an invisible hand." Then, with a wave of the free market magic wand, they assert the same is true for the tens of thousands of corporations that dominate the twenty-first–century global economy.[101] But while they like to quote Adam Smith on business, they avoid mentioning his support of a tax system where the wealthy pay more:

> The necessaries of life occasion the great expense of the poor. They find it difficult to get food, and the greater part of their little revenue is spent in getting it. The luxuries and vanities of life occasion the principal expense of the rich, and a magnificent house embellishes and sets off to the best advantage all the other luxuries and vanities which they possess. A tax upon house-rents, therefore, would in general fall heaviest upon the rich; and in this sort of inequality there would not, perhaps, be anything very unreasonable. It is not very unreasonable that the rich should contribute to the public expense, not only in proportion to their revenue, but something more than in that proportion.[102]

Why is it "not very unreasonable" for the wealthy (and in using that term, let's include corporations) to pay more of the costs of assuring equal opportunity?

Because they receive more of the wealth that *results* from that opportunity—the dedication and hard work of millions of everyday people.

Theodore Roosevelt, writing a hundred and thirty-five years

later, applied Smith's principle in more detail: "I believe in a graduated income tax on big fortunes, and in another tax which is far more easily collected and far more effective—a graduated inheritance tax on big fortunes, properly safeguarded against evasion, and increasing rapidly in amount with the size of the estate."[103]

A progressive income tax, where rates increase with higher incomes, was first established during the Civil War, when a person earning less than $10,000 a year was taxed at 3 percent while one with an income over $10,000 paid 5 percent. In 1895, the Supreme Court concluded that the income tax was unconstitutional, since it was not apportioned to the states. In 1913, the 16th Amendment to the Constitution was passed, making federal income tax a feature of our tax system.

The maximum rates at which higher incomes have been taxed have varied dramatically (see table).

FEDERAL INCOME TAX IN US HISTORY

1913	7%	Wilson
1918	65%	Wilson—World War I
1926	25%	Coolidge
1934	63%	Franklin Roosevelt
1944	94%	Franklin Roosevelt—World War II
1954	91%	Eisenhower
1964	77%	Johnson
1970	70%	Nixon
1981	50%	Reagan
1987	38.5%	Reagan
1997	39.6%	Clinton[104]

In 2010, the top tax rate is 35 percent for a married couple filing a joint return with taxable annual income over $373,000. (Taxable income is net, after exemptions and deductions.) In fact, the rates actually paid by the highest income Americans are much lower because a substantial percentage of their income comes from the capital gains on long-term investments—which are taxed at a maximum of 15 percent.[105]

Similarly, corporate tax rates have varied widely since their inception in 1909. Top corporate rates were initially 1 percent of taxable income. In 1937, 15 percent; 1952, 52 percent; 1972, 48 percent; 1982, 46 percent; in 2002 and 2010, 35 percent.[106]

What tax rates are fair—for people's income and estates, for corporate profits—is a vital part of a national discussion.

To the extreme Right, any such discussion, like the progressive income tax itself, is un-American, an attempt to undermine the dynamism of the entrepreneurial class, of the "free market." In their view, the twenty-five top hedge fund managers who each received $1 billion in income in 2009 "earned it" all by themselves, *not* because market structures, and public institutions, laws and rules, and, most fundamentally, the work and investments by everyday Americans combined to produce the wealth they enjoy. That's nonsense.

Common sense says that if someone benefits more from the public and private institutions that combine to create wealth, he ought to pay more of the costs to keep everything working. Adam Smith agrees.

Jefferson, Lincoln, and Theodore Roosevelt all understood that economic wealth equals power, that it tends to concentrate, and that concentrated power is dangerous. Checks and balances are essential.

Fundamental to those checks and balances is a moral commitment to the worth, rights, and welfare of all human beings—the cornerstone of the founding of the United States of America. In July 2009, Pope Benedict issued an encyclical on morality and economics. He wrote:

> The conviction that the economy must be autonomous, that it must be shielded from 'influences' of a moral character, has led man to abuse the economic process in a thoroughly destructive way. . . . The Church's social doctrine has always maintained that *justice must be applied to every phase of economic activity*. Political authority also involves a wide range of values which must not be overlooked in the process of constructing a new order of economic productivity, socially responsible and human in scale. . . . *The economy needs ethics in order to function correctly*—not any ethics whatsoever, but an ethics which is people-centered. . . . The entire economy and finance, not just certain sectors, must be used in an ethical way so as to create suitable conditions for human development and for the development of peoples.*

All such proposals to require corporations to bring commerce in line with conscience, markets with morality, will be

---

* Given the gravity of the Church's sex abuse scandal, some may object to citing the Pope's call for morality and justice in the economic order. I disagree. As discussed at the outset, the Founders themselves were tarnished by their sanctioning of human slavery. Despite that glaring failure, we still accept as fully valid the moral ideals they articulated. Italics in original.

attacked as anti-business, contrary to "free markets," and "sound economic policy."

In response, it is fair to ask: Why should business enterprise have the right to pay employees poverty wages, force them to work in dangerous conditions, or pollute our environment? Should they have right to undermine the physical health or moral values of our children? The Pope's encyclical raises that fundamental question. And he says no: Economic enterprise needs to reflect morality and conscience.

There is only one possible argument to be made against him: That commerce cannot function effectively in a moral environment.

Are we as a people, as the American nation, willing to accept that argument? No, we are not. Millions of business people approach their jobs every day with a strong moral code, committed to do what is right for their employees, their customers, and their country. The same is true of workers. In our hearts, we know that morality and conscience are essential to the integrity of all human institutions, including our economy.

Pope Benedict is reinforcing that basic truth—and making clear that major reforms will be needed to achieve "economic productivity, socially responsible and human in scale," based on "people-centered ethics"—the welfare and fulfillment of the human being.

CHAPTER 7

CONSERVATION

Would it not please you to study nature on all her wonderful operations, and to relieve your fellow creatures under the severest pains and distresses to which human nature is liable?

—JOHN ADAMS, LETTER TO HIS SON

Of all the questions which can come before this nation, short of the actual preservation of its existence in a great war, there is none which compares in importance with the great central task of leaving this land even a better land for our descendants than it is for us . . .

—THEODORE ROOSEVELT, 1910

We abuse land because we regard it as a commodity belonging to us. When we see land as a community to which we belong, we may begin to use it with love and respect . . . Conservation is a state of harmony between men and land.

—ALDO LEOPOLD, 1949

In the late 1700s, Thomas Jefferson was concerned about the depletion of soil productivity by poor farming techniques. He advocated alternative practices, and invented a plow to reduce erosion. A century later, America was the first nation in the world to establish national parks. Theodore Roosevelt, the great Progressive pioneer of conservation in America, established our system of national forests and greatly expanded our national parks. T. R. appointed his close friend, Gifford Pinchot, as first chief of the US Forest Service; Gifford defined conservation as "the greatest good, for the greatest number, for the longest term." Today, we might summarize that concept in one word: sustainability. Despite our amazing inventiveness and creativity, we have not yet achieved it. Why? Because we are strongly and naturally inclined to think and act for the immediate, the short term, and, as a consequence, to ignore the combined and long-term consequences of our actions.

This tendency is greatly magnified by corporate pressures for short-term investment return: One day Ted Turner and I were driving on a jeep trail through timbered meadows, and from the thick dark trees came the high-pitched whistles of cow elk calling to their calves. In the distance Turner's American bison dotted part of the 106,000-acre landscape that he had protected with a conservation easement, the largest in the world.

I said to him, "You know a lot of these global CEO guys. They're above average in intelligence, have access to any information they want. They have great economic and political power, live at the top of the pyramid. So they have an interest in the status quo, in stability. They want to maintain their position and pass that on to their kids and grandkids, right?"

"That's fair."

"Two threats jeopardize that. One is global poverty. Poverty-stricken people are volatile. They cause revolutions. Second is environmental destruction—it's global and threatens the world of these guys' grandkids. So why don't they use their influence on both fronts? I don't get it."

Ted Turner has an instant opinion on almost any issue, but he was silent for perhaps five seconds. Then he said, without anger or condemnation, "They don't see past their noses. They live in a world of quarterly reports."

A graphic example was the Deepwater Horizon Gulf oil disaster of 2010. Our global addiction to oil has pushed the corporate world more and more toward the edge of safety in its pursuit. Incentives to cut corners to maximize profit are combined with greater and greater technological risks. The result: We move inexorably closer to catastrophic failures that we can neither anticipate nor contain.

When disaster strikes, we look for someone to blame—bad people, a "bad" corporation, or incompetent regulators. That blame game diverts us from facing the real threat that arises from our failure as a nation, a global community, to end our addiction to cheap energy and its inevitable consequences.

A FALSE DEBATE: NATURE VERSUS HUMAN NEEDS

Since the 1970s there has been a false debate in America about conservation, pitting human needs against the health of the natural world. The argument is false because it is inconceivable that human civilization can exist, let alone flourish, in a world where the basic processes of nature are severely damaged.

People have used and altered the natural world since the dawn of agriculture, some 10,000 years ago. In doing so, we protected ourselves against some forces of nature, but not others. We developed crops, and stored surplus food to insulate us from hunger. But such improvements often come with a price: Disease spread more rapidly among the concentrated human populations of towns and cities. We also lost the mobility of our ancestors: farming is tied to specific places, making us vulnerable to drought and flood. And pre-industrial agricultural life involved backbreaking labor. Most people died by age thirty.

The great promise of the Machine Age was to reduce the toll of hard labor, and to further protect us from the harshness of nature. Philosophers predicted "man's ability to triumph over nature," a view that held through much of the twentieth century. Science and the technology it spawned were seen as tools to conquer nature, to bend it to our will.

And human inventiveness *has* radically altered our lives for the better. We have built spectacular cities. We live, work, and drive in climate-controlled spaces; and we have a wonderfully rich assortment of foods and goods from which to choose. In many parts of the world, machines have replaced harsh manual labor, and water purification, sewage disposal, and modern medical discoveries have more than doubled our life span. We have tapped into the earth's long-stored sources of the earth's energy and unleashed the power of the atom. We have created great art, literature, and music that can be shared instantly around the world.

In doing all these things, we have slowly and painfully learned a central lesson: All life on our planet is interconnected. If we misuse our extraordinary technologies in ways that inflict damage on the earth's natural processes, we jeopardize our own survival.

Every one of us depends ultimately for existence on the processes that produce clean air, water, fertile soil, and life itself. We live at the pinnacle of a pyramid of life forms that are in constant interaction and fully interdependent. Destroy tiny plankton in the sea and the whole ocean food system collapses, taking with it the fish we eat. Cause the climate to warm and pine bark beetle larva are able to survive the winter; they burst forth to destroy millions of acres of northern forests, depriving us of wood products and of the living trees that produce oxygen, stabilize soil, and enable clean-running rivers. There is no escape: The fundamental challenge of our time is to bring the use of our phenomenal, wealth-producing technology into compatibility with the natural world.

Only during the past one hundred years or so we have *begun* to understand the full extent of this interconnectedness and interdependence, the damage we have inadvertently done to it, and the threat this damage poses to us all. In short, we have recently developed the foundations of ecological understanding, and, therefore, the ability to make informed and wise choices. It is an irony of history: Our ancestors' painful, difficult development of agricultural and industrial production severely damaged nature; it also created tremendous economic wealth. That wealth has led to research, knowledge, and education, finally leading to a new and pivotal understanding that we need to change the way we use nature.

CONSERVATION AND POVERTY

Real choice requires knowledge of actual alternatives and the social wealth to absorb potential costs. Poverty-stricken people have no choice: They will do what is needed to survive, and inevitably do serious harm to the natural world. Therefore, we will not be able to achieve environmental health and stability in a world of mass poverty. It follows that economic development *that raises the standard of living of several billion human souls* is essential to preserving the health of the planet.

Measuring economic progress by poverty reduction and equitable distribution of the wealth produced is fundamentally different than the standards used by the advocates of "free markets." They assess the economy by the gross domestic product, status of the stock market, increased labor efficiency, and corporate profit. The quality and quantity of food on people's tables, or our access to health care, or the condition of the natural world are not on their financial reports. Why?

If the ultimate purpose of economic growth is to enhance the quality of human lives, why isn't *distribution* of wealth monitored as carefully as the *production* of wealth? After all, one of the main arguments of proponents of unregulated market forces is that "a rising tide lifts all boats." But they never get around to measuring the "lift"! "Market values" never evaluate wealth distribution, focusing instead on economic indicators that are fully separate from human and environmental impacts.[107] Thus, despite decades of tremendous economic expansion, extensive poverty and environmental degradation continue.

The fact is that today's world has immense discretionary wealth: financial wealth, wealth in research, knowledge and information accessible to billions of intelligent human souls. That wealth creates alternative ways of producing our energy, food, goods, and services. *What we need now are economic structures and incentives that work simultaneously to meet human, environmental, and economic needs.*

Making this transition to what some call the "radical center" will not be simple or easy, but in the effort to achieve it we can unite Americans in working for ethical and profitable business enterprise, conservation, and human justice—a coalition that will provide a potent counterweight to the proponents of quick money, exploitation, and greed.

First, we need to be honest with ourselves: Many actions that damaged the environment were taken with full knowledge. The centuries-old, astoundingly rich cod fishery off America's Atlantic coast was destroyed, despite ample warning that over-fishing would devastate the resource. That story has been repeated thousands of times. And today we continue to see the pattern: Specific parts of nature are viewed as marketable commodities, convertible into profitable products and financial wealth. Used for that purpose, they are often over-exploited, damaging the balance of the whole.

In the late 1980s I visited an open pit, cyanide heap leach gold mine operating on public land near Elko, Nevada. Gigantic machines were busily engaged in destroying an entire mountain. They moved roughly thirty-five tons of rock and soil for every ounce of gold produced. The waste—millions of tons—was hauled onto high ridges and dumped into aspen-filled valleys far below. The scale of the destruction—labeled "reclamation"—was stunning. Gold is a valuable commodity in the jewelry market. The valleys, and the plants and animals that live in them—all owned by the American people—have no value in the global marketplace. Hence this destruction makes "economic sense."

Aldo Leopold was an American farmer and conservationist who understood that we use nature's products to survive. He grew food crops and cut down trees for heat and lumber. And he pondered a great deal about our relationship to the natural world. In his famous book, *A Sand County Almanac*, he wrote: "Conservation is a state of harmony between man and nature. . . . We abuse land because we regard it as a commodity belonging to us. When we see land as a community to which we belong, we may begin to use it with love and respect. There is no other way for land to survive the impact of mechanized man. . . ."

SHORT-TERM PROFIT VERSUS LONG-TERM PRODUCTIVITY

Each year in the United States, *1.2 million acres of farmland* is lost to urban uses.[108] There is nothing wrong with the use of land for human houses. The problem arises in *how* these lands are chosen for development. In today's economy, the overriding criterion is *profitability as determined by short-term market forces*. Decades of emphasizing short-term profit above all other considerations has resulted in the dramatic reduction of our nation's best food-producing soils, a colossal waste of energy, and the undermining of our national security.

Take California's Central Valley: When I was a teenager, the valley produced one quarter of the fruits and vegetables consumed by the entire nation. Its climate and Class I soils remain unsurpassed for food production. In the 1960s I drove for hours through prosperous Valley farms. In 2003 I made the same drive. Virtually nothing is left of the farms and agricultural land—it is cookie-cutter subdivisions and shopping malls.

Certainly, we need new housing and businesses to serve a growing nation. But what sort of logic encourages that growth to occur on some of the world's rarest, most productive soils?

In a world of 6.5 billion people, how can it make sense to destroy millions of acres of the globe's best food-producing land? Is it in the long-term interest of the United States to do so? Clearly, it is not. Remaining the world's leading producer of food is a national security issue. Yet under the current rules of the economic game, short-term return on investment trumps even national security.

Our changing climate is the ultimate example of this reality. For years, a coalition of free market "conservatives" and corporations that profit from the use of fossil fuels have denied that human-induced climate change is a problem. Yet overwhelming scientific evidence demonstrates that industrially generated carbon dioxide (CO_2) has altered the balance that maintains our planet's temperature, with potential catastrophic consequences. So why the continued denial by free market fundamentalists and the extreme Right? Because the *reality* of global warming poses a fundamental challenge to their secular religion: "Private enterprise is good; government regulation is an infringement of individual liberty." Since climate change demands new public regulation of some elements of private corporate enterprise, its very existence must be denied.

To honorably address the issue of conservation, we need to face two truths. First, we all depend on resources of the earth—minerals and metals, fiber from trees, food from the soil, water, and air. And having acknowledged our dependence, we need to accept the responsibility to use those natural riches wisely, not to waste them or do irreparable harm to the health of the ecological systems that produce them. We need to accept that responsibility personally, as families, as business people, and as a nation.

Our choices and actions must simultaneously be good for people, and good for the land.

That two-part test sounds simple, but implementing it will not be. We human beings have been making decisions based on short-term expediency for a long time, and today we are all dependent to some degree on economic institutions that emphasize the short term.

USING MARKET FORCES

In approaching change, we need to understand that one of the most creative and effective tools at our disposal is market forces. This book has criticized markets as they often function today: short-term profit at the expense of important community interests. But given the right "rules of the road," markets are wonderfully efficient at allocating resources, responding to customer choice, and minimizing costs. The essential problem in our present use of market forces is confusion between means and ends. As Amory Lovins has put it, "Markets are a wonderful tool, a terrible master, and a worse religion." By putting rules and incentives in place to assure that market forces enhance, rather than undermine, important values, we can maximize their benefits to society.

Food provides an important example: Americans are increasingly concerned about the health effects of industrially grown foods that rely heavily on use of herbicides, pesticides, and fossil fuels and they are responding in a positive way. Despite hundreds of millions of dollars spent to subsidize and promote industrial and pre-fab foods, we have been changing our eating habits. From 1997 to 2006, US organic food sales increased by 80 percent.[109] A decade earlier, it was considered boutique yuppie food. Today, major marketers like Costco, Safeway, and Wal-Mart offer organic lines. "Natural" foods, a broader category produced with sustainable agricultural practices and without preservatives, are likewise skyrocketing in market share. In food, informed customer choice is driving progressive change, and markets respond and deliver the goods.

Additionally, many communities are working to recreate "local food systems" to replace or supplement the multinational industrial model. In the United States the average tomato is estimated to travel 1,500 miles to get to the person who eats it. In a world of expensive and global-warming energy use, that makes no sense.

Coalitions of farmers, ranchers, and customers have developed an expanding network of farmers' markets, where farmers sell directly to consumers, as well as "farm-to-school" and "farm-to-college" programs, where farmers sell directly to these institutions.

The policy arguments are compelling.

- Local food is typically fresher, better tasting, and more nutritious; much of it is grown with sustainable methods.

- Food dollars stay in the community, circulating to produce more jobs; farmers and ranchers increase their profits by eliminating middlemen.

- Less fossil fuels are used to grow and ship food.

- And, yes, local food systems are far less vulnerable to the threat of terrorist attack.

There is something else: customers and growers *talk* with each other—about the weather, kids, the ball game—just as in the small grocery where I had my first job. The development of local food systems reflects rediscovery of market economics that rebuilds our sense of community. And they're good business.

CHAPTER 8

THE AMERICAN CONSCIENCE

I believe the declaration that "all men are created equal" is the great fundamental principle upon which our free institutions rest.

—ABRAHAM LINCOLN, 1858

Whatever America hopes to bring to pass in the world must first come to pass in the heart of America.

—DWIGHT D. EISENHOWER, 1953

I beg you. Look for the words "social justice" or "economic justice" on your church web site. If you find it, run as fast as you can. . . . Am I advising people to leave their church? Yes!

—GLENN BECK, 2010

When we look back on the unique history of our nation, we see many things about which we can feel justly proud. Our Founding principles inspired the colonists to challenge the world's most powerful empire, and they have stood the test of time, giving people around the world the hope that we would all one day live in a world of human freedom, equality, democracy, and justice.

There are long, dark chapters as well. As honorable people we must face squarely the tragic list: enslavement of Africans, extermination of Native Americans, oppression of women, and grim exploitation of sharecroppers, migrant laborers, immigrants, industrial workers, even children. Each of these tragedies represents a betrayal of the American conscience. It continues today in our national acceptance that one out of seven Americans live in poverty in the richest nation in the history of the world, and, at home and abroad, allowing short-term corporate interests to override the rights of everyday people.

What separates the bright chapters from the dark is the American conscience, and the actions we have taken as a people to honor it.

"WITH LIBERTY AND JUSTICE FOR ALL"

Each person reading this book has said the Pledge of Allegiance a thousand times, ending with the words "with Liberty and Justice for all." But we seldom reflect on what those words have meant in the life of our nation, and mean today. We need to.

The Founders were divided on the issue of slavery. Then as now, property rights extremists argued that the right to own property was superior to the fundamental human rights inscribed in the Declaration of Independence. That was the slave owners' argument in support of the right to own, buy, sell, and sexually abuse other human beings, and they backed it up with violence and murder. Looking back, we find this incredible. How could seemingly honorable, educated, rational men defend human enslavement? Were they normal human beings blinded by the economic and personal power that slavery gave them?

To get the votes needed to ratify the Constitution, the Founders agreed to postpone resolution of the issue, and so the

Constitution sanctioned slavery.[110] The southern states fought for decades to preserve the property rights of slave owners, and were willing to destroy the United States of America to preserve them. It took the Civil War and 600,000 American lives before we finally were able to abolish slavery and preserve our nation, "conceived in Liberty, and dedicated to the proposition that all men are created equal."

Forty-five years after the end of that war, Teddy Roosevelt wrote:

> One of the chief factors in progress is the destruction of special privilege. The essence of healthy liberty has always been, and must always be, to take from some one man or class of men the right to enjoy power, or wealth, or position, or immunity, which has not been earned by his service to his or their fellows. That is what you fought for in the Civil War, and that is what we strive for now.
>
> At many stages in the advance of humanity, this conflict between the men who possess more than they have earned and the men who have earned more than they possess is the central condition of progress.[111]

In 1868, resisting southern attempts to deny equal rights to former slaves, the Fourteenth Amendment to the Constitution was passed: ". . . Nor shall any state deny to any person the equal protection of the laws."

In 1922, the United States Constitution was finally amended to guarantee women the right to vote. Until that time they had been second-class citizens, in many states unable to enter into contracts, or even to own or inherit property. The year 1922 seems like ancient history to many, but my mother was then ten years old. She did not understand it at the time, but thanks to decades of work by women and men committed to the Founders' ideals and the American conscience, she would grow up with a basic right of American citizenship, an unalienable right of a human being.

Prodded by women's organizations and labor unions, individual states passed legislation mandating free public education and abolishing child labor. In combination, these steps opened the doors of opportunity and advancement across class lines to an extent unprecedented in our history.

THE NEW DEAL

In 1929 the stock market crashed, and the Great Depression began. Millions lost their jobs, homes, farms, and businesses. Banks shut down, causing millions more to lose life savings. In response to this crisis of capitalism, conservatives like President Herbert Hoover held steady, maintaining the "business first" policies of the government. The crisis deepened. Elected in a landslide, Franklin Roosevelt took a different path. He launched the New Deal, whose underlying principle was that the federal government must become an active force helping everyday people; and that the great centers of private enterprise needed to be regulated to assure that their immense power was used to enhance, rather than harm, the welfare of the nation. In words that echo powerfully today, FDR said, "a small group had concentrated into their own hands almost complete control over other people's property, other people's money, other people's labor—other people's lives." He added, "Government controlled by money is as great a threat as Government controlled by mobs."

The New Deal saw the establishment of Social Security, the first step to assuring that people would not be destitute after a lifetime of work.[112]

Congress passed legislation establishing a federal minimum wage, a forty-hour work week with additional pay for overtime, and the right of workers to organize unions to bargain for better wages and working conditions. Major business enterprises, including banks and the stock market, were placed under federal regulation to assure stability and enhanced public disclosure. People's savings accounts were for the first time insured by the federal government. Those reforms laid the foundation for decades of economic prosperity.

WORLD WAR II

In the 1940s, still under the leadership of FDR, the United States forged the World War II coalition to fight fascism. Hitler's and Mussolini's ideology explicitly rejected the Enlightenment views of the Founders, and proclaimed democracy a "putrid corpse." Fascists believed that personal freedom, human equality, and equal justice reflected spiritual weakness, and advocated "national blood," "survival of the fittest," and the inherited "will of superior races." They saw war as the highest expression of national character, the means to subjugate inferior people and cultures.

Between 60 and 80 million human lives, including 300,000

Americans and 26 million Russians, died in the fight to defeat fascism. Why? Because, during most of the 1930s, conservatives in Europe and United States claimed that fascism was not a threat, that "we can do business with Hitler."[113]

Franklin Roosevelt understood what fascism stood for, and that it had to be confronted and defeated. The United States led the anti-Hitler coalition, stepping forward as the Arsenal of Democracy, supplying England, Russia, and China with weapons, clothes, and food for millions of people. We fought for the principles enshrined by our Founders, and with our allies we won. The global goodwill we earned lasted for decades.

ENDING SEGREGATION

In the 1950s the American conscience finally began to face the racism embedded deeply in our nation. For decades, southern Democrats and "states' rights" conservatives in Congress had protected racial segregation and the legally enforced subjugation of black Americans. With politicians unwilling to face up to this betrayal of American values, the United States Supreme Court acted. In 1954, in *Brown v. Board of Education*, the Court ruled that segregated schools were inherently unequal, and therefore violated the Constitution. Southerners resisted, often resorting to violence. Led by demagogues like Senator James Eastland of Mississippi, Arkansas Governor Orville Faubus, Alabama Governor George Wallace, and South Carolina Senator Strom Thurmond, white supremacists fought against racial equality. They attacked and beat African Americans who tried to vote; if necessary, they murdered them. They shot men down in front of their families; they lynched them in front of jeering crowds; and they bombed churches. In the 1960s, when thousands of white northerners went south to help blacks in their struggle, the white supremacists attacked and killed them, too.

But America's conscience was finally aroused, and in 1964 Congress passed the Civil Rights Act, which banned segregation in interstate commerce, including hotels, restaurants, and public transportation. Forcing blacks to "ride in the back of the bus," drink from separate water fountains, and use "colored only" bathrooms became a violation of federal law. A year later, the Voting Rights Act was passed. The devious tools used to keep southern blacks from voting were removed. The conscience of America had spoken.

Resistance to equal rights was done to preserve privilege, by people who considered themselves better than others. They claimed to be conservatives and patriots, proclaimed their loyalty to the Constitution, the Pledge of Allegiance, "states' rights," the American flag, and even Almighty God. In fact, they rejected America's Founding principles and subverted our central ideals.

MEDICARE

In 1965 Medicare was passed, assuring that American seniors would have access to quality health care. Free market "conservatives" labeled the program an attack on free enterprise. Ronald Reagan called it socialism.

Before the passage of Social Security and Medicare, senior citizens had the highest rate of poverty of any age class in

America. With the programs now in place, their poverty rate is the lowest in the nation.

PROTECTING OUR ENVIRONMENT

The 1970s saw the American conscience turn to the environment as citizens became aware of the damage unregulated industry was doing to the natural world. I live in Montana, a state renowned for its wild lands and natural beauty, a state which had suffered severely through decades of unregulated mining and logging. In 1972, citizen delegates assembled to draft a new state constitution. At the beginning of the document, they adopted a Declaration of Rights. Under Inalienable Rights, they wrote:

> All persons are born free and have certain inalienable rights. They include the right to a clean and healthful environment and the rights of pursuing life's necessities, . . . acquiring and protecting property, and seeking their safety, health and happiness in all lawful ways. In enjoying these rights, all persons recognize corresponding responsibilities.

The right to a clean and healthful environment was the first of its kind in any state constitution in the nation.

At the federal level our environmental rights as citizens gained recognition, too. The Clean Water and Clean Air Acts were passed to restore these foundations of life and to protect them for future generations. "Free market" advocates claimed these laws would damage business, drive up prices, and infringe on private property rights. More than three decades later, despite repeated attempts to repeal them, these laws enjoy strong support of the American people.

THE RIGHTS OF WOMEN

Also in the 1970s, the American conscience focused on discrimination against women. Passed by Congress in 1972, Title IX banned discrimination against women in any educational program receiving federal funding. In high school and intercollegiate athletic programs, funding went overwhelmingly to men's programs, with women getting the leftovers. One of the law's consequences was to require equal funding for women's athletics. I was the men's varsity boxing coach at the University of California at the time, and remember the outcry from male colleagues. The new law, they said, would gut their budgets and destroy intercollegiate sports. They directed their anger not at the injustice long endured by women, but at the attempt to establish equality.

Title IX has enabled generations of young American women to experience high-caliber athletic competition, including the power of teamwork, the pain and reward of pushing to the physical limit and beyond, the facing of doubt and fear, the drive to be one's very best. Thanks to the American conscience, every young woman in the nation now has that opportunity.

And the United States Supreme Court ruled in *Roe v. Wade* that a pregnant woman enjoyed the right of privacy under the United States Constitution, and that right enabled her to choose, under specific conditions, whether or not to terminate her pregnancy. *Roe v. Wade* struck down laws in many states that made criminals of women who chose abortion, and doctors who performed them.

In the 1980s, Congress passed the Americans with Disabilities Act to help assure that disabled citizens had access to public facilities and could not be discriminated against in seeking or holding a job. For far too long, we had ignored the hardships they faced and had looked the other way. Finally, the American conscience said, no, we need to do something honorable. And we did.

For decades, many state laws made same-sex acts by consenting adults a felony. In Montana, for example, the prescribed punishment was up to ten years in prison and a $50,000 fine.[114] In 2003, the United States Supreme Court struck down such statutes as a violation of the Constitution's guarantee of equal protection under the law.

Spanning a hundred and fifty years of our nation's history, these triumphs for economic and social justice breathed life into the words, "with Liberty and Justice for all." Each was controversial in its time. Each was initiated and fought for by an alliance of liberal and progressive Americans; and every one of them was vehemently, even violently, opposed by the American Right, by people who applied to themselves the label "conservative." In every case, it required organized citizens acting according to American conscience, taking risks, doing the hard work to bring America closer to its stated ideals.

The meaning of words, including political labels, changes with time. That being said, why is it that, in every one of these cases, self-described conservatives rose in opposition? From the American Revolution through the Abolition Movement and

Civil War, from child labor to women's right to vote, with Social Security, civil rights, Medicare, and laws to protect our environment, conservatives of the time stood firmly on the wrong side of history. Again and again, they put privilege and property rights above universal freedom, economic and social justice, and human equality.

It is fair to ask those who claim the conservative label today how they regard each of these historic manifestations of the American conscience. Do they support them? If not, why not? If so, how do they reconcile that support with opposition to today's proposals to move toward more equal distribution of opportunity and wealth, to insure equal rights, and to protect the environment?

As for the overwhelming majority of Americans, who among us does not take pride in these historic accomplishments, knowing in our hearts that each of these actions reflects the Founders' commitment to justice?

HUMAN RIGHTS

In reviewing how the American conscience has spoken over time to implement the Founders' vision, we have really been exploring how as a nation we have come to define two words: human rights.

The Founders were serious students of history. They had read the Classics; they had studied the histories of Greece and Rome and understood how the concepts of democracy, government, and the rights and duties of citizens had developed there. They were disciples of the Enlightenment, which held that human beings were endowed with a moral compass, and with the capacity to develop and refine that morality through reason. They had read the great French philosophers. And so, when they wrote and adopted the Declaration of Independence, they made clear they were not simply appealing to an American audience: The Declaration's first sentence includes the phrase, "a decent respect for the opinions of mankind requires" that they should state their case for independence. And they were not simply writing about Americans. They wrote "All men are created equal, that they are endowed by their Creator with certain unalienable rights, that among these are Life, Liberty and the pursuit of Happiness. . . ." That is why Lincoln said that the Declaration had given "hope to all the world, for all future time."

In the Bill of Rights, the Founders further expanded on the rights guaranteed to all citizens, including freedom of speech, press, assembly, religion, the right to bear arms, and the right to a speedy and fair trial before a jury of one's peers. These, and the other rights they listed, were not meant to be a complete list—just those specifically guaranteed by the Constitution. For example, the Founders clearly believed in the right of privacy, but they did not explicitly describe it in the Bill of Rights.

The Declaration and the Bill of Rights, like the Magna Carta before them, have had profound influence over time, as peoples around the world developed their own constitutions, enriching on a global scale the concept of human rights.

From 1939 to 1945, World War II raged on as the most devastating war in history. The wonders of science and technology were used to implement mass slaughter. It was no accident that war had been launched by men who rejected the philosophy of the Enlightenment. The fascist and Nazi beliefs in national and racial supremacy, and in violence and war as the virtuous expression of that supremacy, gave them no qualms about killing people of other nations and races, who they considered "subhuman." They bombed and machine-gunned them from the air as they fled the zones of war. They forced them to dig their own graves and shot them down. When they captured them on the battlefield they locked them in open enclosures and let them starve or freeze to death, while mocking them for their "animal-like" nature. And they built factories to murder them.

In his 1941 State of the Union speech, President Roosevelt called for protection throughout the world of "Four Freedoms": freedom of speech, freedom of conscience, freedom from fear, and freedom from want. The Four Freedoms became the moral foundation of the Allied war effort against fascism. When the war ended, the world was horrified to learn the true nature and scale of the atrocities committed. Led by the government of the United States, they decided to work to prevent it from ever happening again. The creation of the United Nations was the result. Its Charter "reaffirms faith in fundamental human rights, and dignity and worth of the human person," and committed all member nations to promote "universal respect for, and observance of, human rights and fundamental freedoms for all without distinction as to race, sex, language or religion."

But many felt that statement was too general, and pushed for an internationally accepted and detailed statement of just what "human rights" means in the modern world.

The UN Commission on Human Rights was chaired by Eleanor Roosevelt, widow of the president and without question the most well-known and respected woman in the world. She played a pivotal role in the development of the Universal

Declaration of Human Rights. Submitted to the UN General Assembly in 1948, it was adopted unanimously, with forty-eight votes, including that of the United States.[115]

Its preamble reads in part:

> Whereas recognition of the inherent dignity and of the equal and inalienable rights of all members of the human family is the foundation of freedom, justice and peace in the world,
>
> Whereas disregard and contempt for human rights have resulted in barbarous acts which have outraged the conscience of mankind, and the advent of a world in which human beings shall enjoy freedom of speech and belief and freedom from fear and want has been proclaimed as the highest aspiration of the common people. . . .
>
> Now, Therefore, THE GENERAL ASSEMBLY proclaims THIS UNIVERSAL DECLARATION OF HUMAN RIGHTS as a common standard of achievement for all peoples and all nations. . . .

The Declaration includes the rights of the individual as a person, and as a member of society, following our Bill of Rights and adding additional provisions, including:

> All human beings are born free and equal in dignity and rights. Everyone has the right to:
> - life, liberty and security of person;
> - equality before the law and is entitled to equal protection of the law;

- presumption of innocence when charged with a crime, and a public trial at which he has had all the guarantees necessary for his defense;
- ownership of property, alone or with others;
- freedom of thought, conscience and religion; this right includes freedom to . . . in public or private, to manifest his religion or belief in teaching, practice, worship and observance;
- freedom of opinion and expression, peaceful assembly and association; and participation in the government of his country, directly or through freely chosen representatives. The will of the people shall be the basis of the authority of government.
- No one shall be subjected to torture or to cruel, inhuman or degrading treatment or punishment.
- The family is the natural and fundamental group unit of society and is entitled to protection by society and the State.

The Declaration also includes economic and social rights:

- Everyone, as a member of society, has the right to social security and is entitled to . . . the economic, social and cultural rights indispensable for his dignity and the free development of his personality.
- Everyone has the right to work, to free choice of employment, to just and favorable conditions of work and to protection against unemployment. Everyone, without any discrimination, has the right to equal pay for equal work. Everyone who

works has the right to just and favorable remuneration ensuring for himself and his family an existence worthy of human dignity, and supplemented, if necessary, by other means of social protection.

▪ Everyone has the right to form and to join trade unions.

▪ Everyone has the right to a standard of living adequate for the health and well-being of himself and of his family, including food, clothing, housing and medical care and necessary social services, and the right to security in the event of unemployment, sickness, disability, widowhood, old age or other lack of livelihood in circumstances beyond his control. Motherhood and childhood are entitled to special care and assistance.

▪ Everyone has the right to education. Education shall be free, at least in the primary grades.

▪ Parents have a prior right to choose the kind of education that shall be given to their children.

▪ In the exercise of his rights and freedoms, everyone shall be subject only to such limitations as are determined by law solely for the purpose of securing due recognition and respect for the rights and freedoms of others and of meeting the just requirements of morality, public order and the general welfare in a democratic society.

It's fair to ask: Why should the International Declaration—adopted more than sixty years ago—matter to us today?

Here is why:

The United States was a central force behind the Declaration's drafting and adoption, which took place precisely at the time the Cold War was taking hold. For the next forty-five years of that global struggle, the United States loudly championed the cause of human rights, and consistently criticized the communist nations for failing to honor them. We labeled ourselves and our allies the Free World, and held out our nation to the world's people as champions of human rights *that all people deserve*.

Twenty years after the collapse of the Soviet Union, it is time to take a look in the mirror and ask: Did we really mean it? If so, what promises remain unfulfilled, what work unfinished?

FIGHTING POVERTY IN AMERICA

Perhaps the most difficult internal challenge we face today is the poverty that afflicts roughly one in seven Americans, and one in five of our nation's children. Despite the tripling of the gross domestic product since 1980, the poverty rate in 2007 was 13 percent—before the 2008-09 economic crash. In 2004, the wealthiest 25 percent of US households owned 87 percent of the country's wealth, while the bottom 25 percent held *no net wealth at all*.[116] In 1997, one man, Bill Gates, was worth approximately as much as 40 *million* American households at the low end of wealth distribution.[117]

How is this possible?

There are three parts to the answer: global markets, philosophy, and public policy.

During the past thirty years, the combination of global market forces and tax policy has encouraged concentration of wealth at the top. People of wealth have been able to invest anywhere in the world to capitalize on the most profitable opportunities as they emerge, multiplying their assets. Understandably, they do. Since the 1950s, tax rates on the wealthy have dropped dramatically—both income tax and capital gains tax on investments.[118]

Those tax policies reflect a dominant political philosophy among the political and economic elite. In summary, it is this: The "free market" is the most efficient and fair allocator of wealth, and the entrepreneurial class is the most important, productive part of society. Therefore, government policies that concentrate the wealth and increase the economic power of this group—such as corporate subsidies, low corporate tax rates, and lower taxes on stock investments than on workers' wages—are good. They move wealth "up" the economic pyramid, where it will be spent wisely and invested in the economy. Government policies aimed at moving wealth "down," to lower elements of the pyramid are bad because the people at the bottom are "tax eaters, not taxpayers."[119]

Years ago, I heard Rush Limbaugh for the very first time on the radio. Today, I still remember his calling Americans who lived in poverty "parasites." That view is not new: many people who enjoy privilege and power have throughout history viewed the poor as lazy or lacking in ability, and therefore deserving of their grim economic conditions. If they have little education, or are barely literate, it is because they lack intelligence. If more of their children die at an early age, it is regrettable, but the fault of the parents. If they work for wages that are inadequate to provide food, clothing, and shelter for themselves and their family, they simply are not qualified for higher-paying jobs; the market appropriately pays people exactly what supply and demand determines they are worth.

However, not all of the economic elite see it this way. Down through the generations, principled wealthy people have seen beyond their personal circumstances and given generously to alleviate suffering. Others have committed time, energy, and even their lives to redress the imbalance of wealth and power of their time. Thomas Jefferson was one of those. He understood that wealth and property translated into economic and political power that could be wielded against the interests of the common man. To him, democratic government was an essential and necessary counterbalance.

In 1787, in a letter from France, Jefferson wrote, "Experience declares that man is the only animal which devours his own kind; for I can apply no milder term to the governments of Europe, and to the general prey of the rich on the poor."[120]

In 1792, Tom Paine wrote *The Rights of Man, Part II*. In it, he blamed the European governments of kings and aristocrats for poverty, illiteracy, unemployment, and war. Basic reforms were needed, he argued, and called for representative government, public education, relief for the poor, pensions for the aged, public works for the unemployed, and a progressive income tax to pay the costs. The British government banned the book, jailed its publisher, and indicted Paine for treason.

A century later, in 1884, in the midst of the great industrialization of America, with fantastic fortunes being amassed by a few, the average income of 11 million of the nation's 12 million families was $380 a year. In 1895, the Supreme Court ruled unconstitutional a 2 percent tax on incomes over $4,000. A lawyer friend of Theodore Roosevelt wrote to him, denouncing the tax as "a communist march on private property."[121]

That precise statement could be made today by Glenn Beck, Rush Limbaugh, Ann Coulter, or anyone on the reactionary Right. For them, as for their nineteenth- and twentieth-century ideological mentors, government intervention aimed at reducing poverty through taxes, legislation, or regulation is immoral. Thus, establishing or extending unemployment insurance will only encourage laziness; banning child labor and mandating public education for all children is an infringement on personal liberty and interferes with freedom of contract and the intrinsic wisdom of market forces. For the same reason, no minimum wage should be set by law; if it is, it should never be raised. Public assistance to the poor? It will only produce indolence.

There is a powerful psychological element to this view of the poor: It enables those holding it to feel fully virtuous. There is no moral dilemma if people in poverty are already getting what they deserve. And we help them by *not* helping them: They will learn the value of self-reliance and hard work!*

It is one of our most tenacious human traits to believe what we *want* to believe, to select from among a wide array of facts and arguments those that confirm what we already think. In speeches I sometimes say jokingly, "Everyone who thinks you make too much money, raise your hand." Rarely does a hand go up. Why? In part because we work hard for what we receive. But also, if we felt that we *were* overpaid, it would raise

---

* These same type of self-serving stereotypes were used for centuries by men in relation to women. Women were characterized as emotional, nervous, lacking in judgment and intelligence—and thus unqualified to own or inherit property, work in prestigious professions, obtain a divorce, or vote.

uncomfortable questions: Who is making too little? Why? And what should be done about it?

It is fully human not to like being emotionally uncomfortable, and rationalization—inventing reasons to believe something—is a potent characteristic of the human mind.

Benjamin Franklin, a man with a fine sense of humor, wrote of this quality in himself. He was a vegetarian, but dearly loved the full range of foods. Once when he was traveling by ship, the wind died and the boat floated aimlessly. Passengers began throwing out lines, and catching and then grilling fresh cod. The enticing aroma was too much for Franklin. He tried to focus on his vegetarian objection to eating animals. But the sight and smell of the savory flesh pulled him. So he thought instead about the cod and how they ate other fish. If they ate other life forms, why shouldn't he? And so he had a sumptuous meal, eating his fill of the delicious fish. Then he wrote in his diary: "So convenient a thing it is to be a *reasonable Creature*, since it enables one to find or make a Reason for everything one has a mind to do."[122]

And so it is no surprise that, down through the ages, people who have been fortunate enough to enjoy positions of privilege and power have held to the view that the poor deserve their condition or that there is nothing to be done about it. It is natural human behavior.

There is another reason we struggle with the idea of poverty in America. We are a nation of immigrants, the large majority of whom arrived poor, worked extremely hard, and over generations built a better life. Some of our forebears, through a mixture of ability, hard work, and great luck, became fabulously rich. So we have developed the belief that through hard work, "anybody can make it in America." We take pride in that belief. It makes us feel good about our country.

But there is a fly in that ointment. It is true that out of a thousand people, any one, two or five can become very wealthy. But *everyone* cannot make it. There is exactly room for only 1 percent of the people in the top one percent. The same is true for the top 10 percent and the top 50 percent. We may agree that is fine, but the American sense of fairness has to ask: Is it a level playing field? And what happens to those who don't make it? What sort of living conditions are morally acceptable to us as Americans for the large majority who do not get to the upper rungs?

Additionally, a person's chances of moving up the economic ladder are profoundly influenced by where he or she starts out. If my parents are wealthy and well educated, I am much more likely to go to college and earn a good living than if I was born poor. If my parents live in poverty, my odds of getting rich are slim. According to a study published before the 2008 recession, "only 7% of children born to parents in the bottom wealth quintile (20%) make it to the top wealth quintile as adults."[123]

As a people we take pride in the intrinsic value of each human life. So what do we do if life at the bottom of the economic pyramid is harsh, sharply handicaps people's ability to move up the ladder, and even shortens their lives? It is often more comfortable to deny or ignore that truth. But despite that tendency, gradually and over time, the American conscience, our central belief in fairness, in social and economic justice, has spoken.

In the nineteenth century, workers began to organize unions to push for improved wages and working conditions. Again and again, the power of government was wielded against them, with police and even the military called out to break strikes.[124] Later, democratic government intervened against laissez-faire capitalism with the abolition of child labor, the requirement of mandatory public education for all children, the establishment of Social Security, the forty-hour work week, unemployment insurance, minimum wage,[125] and legislation assuring the right of workers to organize trade unions. Such steps, combined with the economic boom created by World War II and postwar demand, generated the "golden age" of the American economy. Into the 1970s, real incomes of everyday Americans grew dramatically, and a large and vibrant middle class emerged for the first time in our history.

Poverty, was reduced, but not eliminated. In 1959, 22.4 percent of Americans were below the poverty line. In 1964, when President Johnson announced "The War on Poverty," it was 19 percent. He pushed through massive social welfare programs, including Head Start, VISTA, Legal Services for the poor, and others that evolved into the Job Corps, which teaches low-income youth social and vocational skills.

Milton Friedman and other "free market" economists criticized the programs, arguing that pro-business policies would achieve more. But despite cutbacks, many of the programs survived in one form or another and have had a major impact. During the decade that followed, poverty rates fell as low as 11 percent. They ranged from 11 to 15 percent up to 2005, *below one-half the nation's historical average.*[126]

How poverty is defined varies by nation, based on the income needed to meet basic living needs such as food, shelter, and clothing to preserve health. In the United States in 2008-

09, the poverty threshold was calculated as $10,830 for a single person and $22,050 for a family of four.[127] Single-parent families (almost always headed by women) have roughly twice the incidence of poverty as the overall population. Thanks to Social Security and Medicare, senior citizens have the lowest poverty rate of any age group.

In addition to those in poverty, many live close to the line. The plain truth is that the structure of our economy—by far the richest in human history—depends on tens of millions of jobs that pay poverty, or near-poverty wages. Poor people in America often work two jobs and still do not earn enough to pay for rent and food for their families. When that same economy pays executive salaries exceeding $10 million per year, and hedge fund managers *hundreds* of millions per year, you have to ask what's going on.

In 2006, while working on a documentary film, I visited the Chicago factory that makes the famous Academy Award statues. They are perhaps the most glamorous such ornaments in the world. The air-conditioned offices of the R. S. Owens Company were pleasant as the owners described the unique history of the internationally renowned statues, and the high standard of excellence required for their manufacture.

The production area had no air conditioning and was hot and humid. Cinder block walls held woodbins filled with tools and old castings, and "Fire Warning" signs were covered with industrial dust. Furnaces melted gold and platinum as workers—mostly Hispanic—hunched over benches, drills, casting moulds, and polishing wheels. I asked our public relations guide about the wages. "They vary," she said.

Later I found a worker alone and asked what he made.

He hesitated, glancing down the hall. "$12.20 an hour."

He had a wife and two children and had worked at the plant for eighteen years. Another worker told me he had been there twenty-seven years. He made $13.50 an hour.

We visited Las Vegas on the same trip, and I interviewed Mayor Oscar Goodman, former lawyer for the mob. He was, he said, the "happiest mayor of the greatest city in America." He'd come to Vegas with his wife twenty years before, with eighty-seven dollars between them. He was now a wealthy man, the classic rags-to-riches story. He said the city was a wonderful place for working people. "With tips a service worker can bring home $40,000 to $50,000 a year. With a couple working they can buy a home, a swimming pool, achieve the American dream." He was fully confident in his facts.

Back at our hotel I checked with the service workers who cleaned our rooms. They were paid $7.65 an hour, or $15,300 a year, minus payroll deductions.

In another city, hotel workers were picketing. One told me he had worked there for twenty-five years, starting as a janitor and working up to the kitchen. A new corporation had bought the hotel, cut wages by 7.5 percent, and eliminated the employee health insurance program. He had a wife and two children. He said, "You come to this country and work hard, believing in the American Dream. When you fall, it really hurts."

This year, after working late one evening, I headed out of the office building. A man of about thirty was carefully washing the glass front door. He was thin, his body and legs bent by some crippling disease. Still, he was neatly dressed and his hair was carefully combed. I introduced myself and thanked him for the care he was taking in his work.

"I take pride in my work," he said. He spoke clearly, with dignity.

I asked how things were for him in this tough economy.

"Actually, I'm doing all right. A couple of months ago I got laid off at Target. I'd been with them for quite a while, but I had bad back spasms and missed a couple days work. They called and told me not to bother to come back."

I asked what he'd been paid.

"$8.50 an hour. But then I heard about this janitorial contractor and got hired." He smiled. "It's a better job and I get paid more, too."

I did not have the courage to ask what he made now.

In 2009, 980,000 workers received the federal minimum wage of $7.25 an hour. Another 2.6 million were reported as receiving wages below the minimum. In total, these workers comprised almost 5 percent of hourly workers.[128] Between 1979 and 2003, the purchasing power of the minimum wage fell 29 percent.[129]

A major reason that we Americans are uninformed about the real circumstances of working people—above and below the poverty line—is that mainstream media does not tell us about it. Sitcoms, soap operas, and dramas overwhelmingly feature professionals and upper-middle-class families. We naturally assume these accurately portray general life in America. "Reality" police shows do show poor people—usually being arrested for drunkenness, domestic violence, or drug peddling. Our media is almost totally privately owned, and operates to make a profit. It is neither entertaining nor profitable to remind us of the hard realities of much of American life.

And the news? Business news and stock market trends are well covered, as they should be. But how often are we shown the realities faced by a single mother without a high school degree, a minimum wage job, and three kids? Or about the lives of wage earners getting below poverty-line pay? These are the realities of roughly one in four Americans. Wouldn't a truly "balanced media" report on it? Why don't they? Perhaps because it's a downer, and not entertaining. Perhaps because if enough Americans understood the truth, we would insist on change.

In the absence of the facts, it is easy to be misinformed or prejudiced against lower-income Americans.

Here are some facts. To receive Temporary Assistance to Needy Families (TANF), the main welfare program that replaced Aid To Families With Dependent Children in the mid-nineties, you must have minor children, either your own or specific relatives.

There is a five-year lifetime limit for adults.

During this five-year limit, recipients are required to participate in work activities, and are expected to become self-sufficient.

Failure to follow the Work Program rules will lead to a warning, 50 percent benefits reduction, and benefit termination.

Recipients' assets cannot exceed $3,000, including real and personal property. If you live in a house you own, or own a car you need for transportation, these are allowed.

Income cannot exceed allowable standards. In 2010 in Montana, a family of four could not have monthly income greater than $1,299. The maximum monthly benefit payment to your family would be $606. Depending on your income and expenses, it would be less.[130]

Food stamps are available to households whose gross monthly income is 130 percent or less of the Federal poverty guidelines ($2,389 per month for a family of four). In fiscal year 2008, the average monthly food stamp benefit was $101 per person ($25.25 a week) or $227 per household. In fiscal year 2006, 76 percent of all benefits went to households with children, another 16 percent to households including a disabled person, and another 9 percent to households with an elderly person. Most able-bodied adult applicants must meet certain work requirements. Food stamps cannot be used to buy alcohol, cigarettes, any nonfood items, or a meal at restaurant. Undocumented immigrants cannot receive them.[131]

In the absence of the facts, many Americans hold the view that public assistance programs are wasteful and the recipients as lazy.

The truth is that, overwhelmingly, the poor do not *choose* to be poor. Instead, their condition is imposed on them by birth, economic structure, or accident. Whether one's moral code is based on religious faith, or in the simple belief that all people deserve basic human rights, including a fair chance, a fundamental question of conscience looms: Knowing the facts about poverty, what do we *do* about it?

We Americans debate intensely the morality of a pregnant woman terminating her pregnancy. Fair enough. But where is the discussion about our moral duty to the children who are born? Do we or do we not have an obligation to help the one out of five of our nation's children who are born into poverty—with access to a nutritious diet, health care, and quality education?[132] With our phenomenally productive technology and unparalleled wealth, is it acceptable to the American conscience that many regularly skip meals to make ends meet? That 4 or 5 percent unemployment—workers looking for a job, but unable to find one—plus an equal number working part time but seeking full-time jobs—is considered acceptable by many economists, even "structurally healthy"? Should *any* unemployment be acceptable to us as a global superpower?

We need a national discussion about these questions and potential answers. What if we added tax credits for local businesses to hire workers, and increased tax rates for corporations that export American jobs? Should we provide public-funded jobs in infrastructure, transportation, and conservation for those who cannot find work in the private economy? Should we raise the long-term capital gains tax to that of normal, earned income and invest the proceeds in tax credits for small businesses to help them pay a living wage? Are we willing to increase tax rates—yes, including our own—to achieve that? Should we raise the minimum wage high enough to guarantee that those who work full time will not live in poverty—thus avoiding the need for most taxpayer-funded welfare programs and taxpayer-subsidized health care?

President Franklin Roosevelt once said, "No business which depends for existence by paying less than living wages to its workers has any right to continue in this country." Seventy years later, can we achieve that standard? In 2007, The Center for American Progress published "From Poverty to Prosperity: A National Strategy to Cut Poverty in Half." The strategy recommended twelve steps to cut poverty in half by 2017. Among them were raising the minimum wage to assure that people who work full time are not condemned to poverty, expanding the Earned Income Tax Credit for low-wage earners, and promoting unionization by enacting the Employee Free Choice Act.

Free market advocates will argue that raising the minimum

wage will increase unemployment and generate inflationary pressures. What they are really saying is that poverty wages are essential to the "healthy" functioning of a "free market" economy. They don't say that directly and honestly, because they understand that the American people's sense of fairness and justice would not accept it.

They will also *not* say that allowing businesses to pay poverty wages costs the American taxpayers tens of billions of dollars every year. Why? Because we fund Temporary Assistance to Needy Families, the Supplemental Nutrition Assistance Program (food stamps), and Medicaid. Further, poverty produces higher crime rates—from robbery and burglary to drug dealing and domestic violence. So we all pay for courts, police and an ever-expanding prison system that we can no longer afford.[133]

Setting aside for the moment the human misery involved in all this, why should the American taxpayer pay hundreds of billions of dollars to pay for the consequences of poverty-level wages?

Free market fundamentalists will argue that it's not government's business to interfere with wages paid by the private sector. .

Well, if government has no business establishing a floor for wages, we should abolish the minimum wage. (Many on the Right believe exactly that, but won't say it publicly.) And, yes, it is possible that requiring a living wage would eliminate some jobs or result in marginally increased prices to consumers. The same result occurred no doubt when slavery was abolished.

I don't claim the issue is simple: Many low-income jobs are provided by small businesses with low profit margins. Potential tax credits may be needed by those businesses if wages are increased. The implications for teenagers' employment are also real. But market forces clearly generate tremendous wealth. Unregulated, they also generate economic crises and stark, chronic poverty that saps the moral fiber and economic vitality of our nation. The American conscience demands that we develop a sustained, and multi-faceted response to these issues once and for all.

CHAPTER 9

COMMON GROUND

The sun never shined on a cause of greater worth. . . . Now is the seed time of continental union, faith, and honor.

—TOM PAINE, *Common Sense*, 1776

In our complicated modern civilization, we are so separated from each other, that we forget our interdependence.

—ELEANOR ROOSEVELT, 1934

The time has come to reaffirm our enduring spirit; to choose our better history; to carry forward that precious gift, that noble idea, passed on from generation to generation: the God-given promise that all are equal, and all deserve a chance to pursue their full measure of happiness.

—BARACK OBAMA, Inaugural Address, 2009

In fall 2008, more than 80 percent of Americans said the nation was heading in the wrong direction.[134] Without doubt, the election of Barack Obama was a statement by the American people that we needed to change that direction. In the midst of two wars, with the country facing economic collapse and soaring deficits, many of us felt frustration and disappointment. We need to remind ourselves now of the hard truth that change takes much more than the efforts of any one person, and that triumphs of the past required years—sometimes decades—of work by thousands of people committed to shared ideals.

So the question looms: Can we, the citizens of the United States, find common ground to move forward as a nation, and as a leader in the world?

We can, provided we do two things.

1. We must agree on the basic principles to guide our actions.

2. Based on those principles, we must develop an agenda for action that is both practical and moral.

I have given the speech that is the basis of this book more than forty times, and people respond. When I speak about what the gratuitous sex and graphic violence on television is doing to our kids, people nod, their eyes on mine. After the talk, a banker comes up to me. He pauses, his face troubled, "You know, in my job I used to be able to consider personal character in making a loan. Now it's all corporate. We have to judge everything by the numbers; character doesn't count." A nurse steps up, tells me about her anguish and anger at watching the quality of care of sick people determined by their ability to pay. A man thanks me and says, "You said a lot of things I have been feeling, but couldn't quite put into words." Many people say, "There's a lot in that talk to think about." It is disturbing to hear that: If we had not lost our moral sense of direction, there would not be much to think about in my talk.

But we *have* lost our way—amid a baffling array of consumer goods, glitzy advertising, soulless celebrity, and manipulative, fear-driven politics. It is a contradictory truth: the unparalleled wealth that surrounds us is a curse as well as a blessing. Jesus said, "It is as hard for a rich man to get to heaven as it is for a camel to go through the eye of a needle." He was not condemning the wealthy, but instead pointing out how potent is the distraction of wealth, how it deflects us from fundamental truths and moral clarity. We have lost our moral compass in large part because we have become enthralled with the endless pursuit of expensive trinkets and toys. As Lincoln said, "We must disenthrall ourselves, and then we shall save our country."

OUR MORAL COMPASS

We can do that, using founding values as our compass: freedom, responsibility, equality, and justice for all human beings. If we recommit to those principles, if we act on them in our daily lives, in our selection of candidates for public office, and if we apply them in the laws and rules we enact as a democratic community, we will rediscover their power, and recapture our sense of hope and purpose as a nation.

In our fast-changing world, with its pressured and busy lives, can we really come together and actually create change for the better? Isn't there a risk that we will fail and make things even worse?

Those same questions swept across the colonies in 1776. People said, "True, things could be better. But our colonial system has lasted a long time and produced many benefits; we live well. Washington, Jefferson, and the other radicals are crazy. Sticking with the Empire is certainly better than going to war against the greatest military power in history for some idealist concept of independence!"

Many Americans shared that view. But some did not, and on July 4, 1776, their leaders gathered in Philadelphia and placed their signatures under a Declaration of Independence that said in part that "governments are instituted among men to secure these rights, and derive their power from the consent of the governed."

To establish and secure such a government, an eight-year War of Independence was fought.

And won.

CONFRONTING FEAR

Americans had faced the fear of the unknown and held fast. To deal with the problems we face today will require us again to confront fear of the unknown, and of change, and the false fears fanned by the reactionary Right to drown out civic discussion and hamstring democratic government. Fifty million Americans without health insurance? The Right shouts, "death panels!" "government takeover!" "socialized medicine!" Eight and a half million Americans lose their jobs due to unregulated greed and the federal government wants to stimulate the economy by funding work projects? "Socialism!" The planet's climate is warming, threatening a rolling disaster. Global cooperation is needed to combat it. "Conspiracy!" "World Government!"

We will need to stay focused, and recognize propaganda for what it is, and overcome fear.

America faced a terrible crisis during the Great Depression: The economy had collapsed, and almost one worker in three was out of a job. The scale of the disaster was massive, and a paralysis of spirit gripped the nation: "What can we do? We have no power to affect the overwhelming economic forces that have brought calamity upon us."

Franklin Roosevelt understood that paralysis, and its underlying fear. In his First Inaugural Address he confronted the issue head on: "Let me assert my firm belief that the only thing we have to fear is fear itself."

Roosevelt knew personally about fear. He was a child of privilege, raised in wealth and power. He was handsome, brilliant, athletic, attractive to women, his future assured. Then, in his twenties, polio struck him down. He believed he would recover and resume his anointed path to power. But his legs remained crippled and he came to understand he might never walk again. He had to face the fear of losing everything by which he had defined himself as a man. Eventually, he was able to face that fear, in part because he spent time with polio-afflicted children. He saw their undimmed sense of hope, joy, and optimism. He saw their courage. He saw that they did not complain or give up, but instead pushed on. He saw how, despite their loss, they relished life. With their help and inspiration, Franklin Roosevelt overcame his own deepest fears. When his time came, he was able to reach out to a fearful nation and chart a moral course for action and inspire it to respond. He lay out his moral vision in his first inaugural speech in 1933:

> Stripped of the lure of profit by which to induce our people to follow their false leadership . . . they know only the rules of a generation of self-seekers. They have no vision, and when there is no vision the people perish.
>
> The money changers have fled from their high seats in the temple of our civilization. We may now restore that temple to the ancient truths. The measure of the restoration lies in the extent to

which we apply social values more noble than mere monetary profit.

Happiness lies not in the mere possession of money; it lies in the joy of achievement, in the thrill of creative effort. The joy and moral stimulation of work no longer must be forgotten in the mad chase of evanescent profits. These dark days will be worth all they cost us if they teach us that our true destiny is not to be ministered unto, but to minister to ourselves and our fellow men.

Franklin Roosevelt led America through the Great Depression. I grew up twenty years after the Depression and the war, but I learned about it by talking to the parents of my childhood friends. They were liberals and conservatives, Republicans and Democrats. Almost across the board, when I asked about FDR, they said the same thing: "He gave us hope."

Near the end of his life, Martin Luther King, Jr. said:

> I am convinced that if we are to get on the right side of the world revolution, we as a nation must undergo a radical revolution in values. We must rapidly begin the shift from a "thing-oriented" society to a "person-oriented" society. When machines and computers, profit motives and property rights are considered more important than people, the giant triplets of racism, materialism, and militarism are incapable of being conquered.[135]

Men and women like these were able to inspire our nation because they understood what was most dear to our hearts—the unique inheritance of American citizenship, offering both opportunity and responsibility, and aspiring toward freedom and justice for all. They also trusted in our ability to act, to right our wrongs, and to make the world a better place for future generations. We need to do that now.

A PLAN FOR ACTION

First: Let's put the people's government to work again to help secure our rights of life, liberty, and the pursuit of happiness. Today, huge amounts of money pre-select who gets elected to political offices and whose interests they represent. Unless that money warp is fixed, all of our other efforts will fail. So, first and foremost, we must:

- Institute fundamental campaign finance reform to end the control that special interest money exercises over our democracy.

Second: Demand media reform. In today's America, our TV programming is almost purely a conscienceless corporate enterprise. The results—rampant sex and violence, vacuous "entertainment" and ideological "news"—are a disaster for us, for our children, and the nation. Media has the right to make money, but it must also fulfill the Founders' expectation that it strengthen informed citizenship and enhance our democracy. To achieve that end we must:

- Tax national TV advertisements that use the public air-waves, in order to create the American Values Fund, initiating world-class programming for children, teens, parents, and seniors and providing genuine news and public service information worthy of America's citizens.

Third: We need to come together in a national commitment to:

- Assure a top-quality education for all of America's children.

Here again, American moral values and hard-nosed practical reality share common ground: In the knowledge-based global economy of the twenty-first century, our nation cannot prosper without a world-class education system.

Throughout our history, we have pursued that vision. The Founders believed that education was essential to full citizenship and "the pursuit of happiness." For decades, the American people have understood that education was central to the wellbeing of the nation, and willingly funded our public schools, from K-12 to colleges and universities. In 1862, during the darkest hours of the Civil War, Abraham Lincoln signed into law the Morrill Act, giving 6.3 million acres of federal land to the states to enable them to finance the establishment of public, land-grant colleges. The purpose? To insure that everyday Americans across the nation had access to higher learning. Idealism fit with pragmatism: The industrializing nation needed educated minds as well as skilled hands. In 1890, Congress began to make regular appropriations to fund the colleges. Since admission standards there were more open than at private colleges, women, working class students, and students from remote rural regions were able to receive higher education at low cost.

In 1944, during World War II, President Franklin Roosevelt signed into law the Servicemen's Readjustment Act, commonly called the GI Bill of Rights. It provided for college or vocational education for our returning soldiers, a year's unemployment insurance, and subsidized home and business loans. It represented major government intervention in the economy on behalf of everyday people—a huge government "give-away program" and gross violation of "free market principles."

The result? By the time the original GI Bill ended in July 1956, 2.4 million veterans had home loans backed by the Veterans' Administration, fueling economic growth, and 7.8 million World War II veterans had participated in an education or training program. Many were able to move beyond the economic class into which they were born, contributing to the well-being and dynamism of the nation.[136]

The same is true of enabling higher education for low-income people. Roughly 44 million American live below the poverty line; another 57 million earn between $20,000 and $40,000 a year. Higher education dramatically increases income for people in such circumstances. Example: Poverty-level women who were admitted to New York University between 1970 and 1972 were surveyed thirty years later. High school graduates earned an average of $30,000; women who had earned a BA, $42,000, and those with graduate degree $54,500—an 81 percent increase.[137] More than 70 percent of the women who had been given the opportunity earned some kind of degree. And their children enjoyed higher academic success than those of parents from the same community who did not go to college.

Clearly, broadening access to college education is good for American families, the economy, and the nation.

But to get to college, Americans need a quality K–12 education. Right now as a nation we deserve a failing grade:

- An astonishing percentage of American students are no longer proficient in reading and math. An analysis of 2009 national tests found only 12 percent of African-American fourth grade boys are proficient in reading, and only 38 percent of white fourth grade boys. For the same groups in the eighth grade, math proficiency rates were 12 percent and 44 percent respectively.[138]

- Kids from families in the lowest 20 percent of income are six times as likely as those in the top 20 percent to drop out of high school.[139]

- America used to have the greatest number of 25-36 year-olds with college degrees. In 2010, we ranked twelfth out of thirty-six nations.[140]

A few years ago I interviewed George Dennison, president of the University of Montana. We discussed how state legislatures across the nation were cutting back funding for higher education. Dennison said this reflected a fundamental shift in public thinking. In the 1970s, opinion polls showed that roughly 70 percent of Americans felt the primary beneficiary of higher education was the nation as a whole, which benefited from the work and contributions of college graduates. As a result, they were willing to pay the majority of the costs through taxes. Thirty years later the thinking had changed. A majority of Americans now felt the primary beneficiary of college was the graduate, who would make more money in the job market and therefore should pay the cost. The result: Even at public universities, students commonly must incur $20,000 in debt to graduate; at private schools it is commonly twice that or more.

This "privatization" of our thinking—our loss of awareness that our public investments are directly related to our own well-being and that of our community—has had dire results: A student's cost for a college education has skyrocketed, increasingly eliminating lower- and middle-income Americans; their brainpower is lost to the nation. When I interviewed Dennison again just before his retirement in 2010, he said that our K–12 schools were failing to prepare our children for college: "We are abandoning our longstanding social contract to educate our children. This will be the first generation of Americans who are less well educated than their parents."

A broad consensus exists from educators, parents, the business community, and political leaders that we must reverse this trend, and return our public school system to its mission of achieving excellence. Proposals for change that have gained broad support include increasing federal aid to states—tied to tough requirements for improvement:

- Comprehensive tracking of each student's performance;

- Enhanced pay for teachers and accountability for student progress;

- Longer school hours and more school days;

- State action plans to confront failing schools;

- Encouraging on-the-ground learning out in the community;

- Generating stronger parental engagement and support.

But achieving a world-class education for all America's children will cost money. Even with much-needed reforms in our tax code, will each of us have to pay more?

Damn right.

These three reforms—of our electoral system, mass media, and public education—will lay the foundation for a national renewal based on the engaged, informed citizenry that the Founders envisioned. They will change the rules of the game that have given control of our government and our media to narrow, selfish interests. And they will level the playing field of American democracy. *In sum, they will allow our democracy to function as the Founders intended, and enable us to seek real solutions to the central challenge of our time:*

- We need to improve the structure of our economy to preserve its phenomenal capacity to produce wealth and at the same time ensure it benefits *all the people* who make it function, and sustains the health of our planet.

HEALTH CARE AND PERSONAL RESPONSIBILITY

The United States has been a leader in many areas of human rights, but in the area of health care we have fallen far behind. Ours is the richest society in history, yet in 2009, nearly 50 million Americans, including 9 million children, had no health insurance. According to the Institute of Medicine, lack of health care coverage causes the unnecessary deaths of 18,000 Americans a year.[141]

The 2009 health reform legislation is designed to provide coverage for 93 percent of Americans, ban lifetime caps on insurance coverage, and make it illegal for insurance companies to cancel coverage when someone gets ill. These are important steps, but even the legislation's supporters acknowledge that much more needs to be done to rein in runaway costs. American health care costs now approach $8,000 per person per year, roughly twice as much as other advanced nations—and the price is increasing at twice the rate of inflation. It now consumes 17 percent of our gross domestic product, an extraordinary sum.[142] Our results in treating key major diseases are no better, or even worse, than other countries. Part of the problem is "fee for service medicine" whose perverse incentives lead to unnecessary treatments and drive up costs.[143] It must be replaced with the kind of "team approach" and outcome-based financial incentives used by the Cleveland Clinic and other leading hospitals.

But there is another, simpler element: basic personal responsibility. All too often when we encounter a problem, we've fallen into the trap of finding someone else to blame. The fact is, a lot of us Americans are simply not working at eating well, staying healthy, and controlling our weight. Our couch potato syndrome is having a devastating impact on our health—and especially on the health of our children.[144] Unless we get off our backsides and regularly start exercising alone or with our friends, and get our kids engaged in athletics and the outdoors, we will face national health care costs that will overwhelm the nation. As parents and citizens, we simply cannot let this happen.

America was the world's leader in conservation for most of the twentieth century. We established hundreds of millions of acres as national parks, forests, and grasslands; and we passed pioneering legislation to restore and preserve clean air and water and protect endangered species. But as in other areas of American life, we have lost our way, trading away needed additional environmental protection for short-term profit.

We need to aggressively develop economic models that work for the long haul—in Gifford Pinchot's words, "the greatest good for the greatest number for the longest term." And in that work America can lead the world.

We can begin with our nation's public lands, which belong to every man, woman, and child in America. In the nineteenth century, our nation had a social contract based on exploration and settlement of the West. For most of the twentieth century, the contract was for extraction of natural resources to fuel the growing nation. But in the process we caused great damage to the land.

▪ It is time for a new social contract of restoration and long-term stewardship of our public lands—to bring our forests, grasslands, and watersheds back to full health, as a perpetual source of clean air and water, abundant wildlife and recreation, and sustainable production of natural resources for this and future generations.

Restoration of our national forests will bring Americans together in common cause. Restoration means replanting trees along thousands of miles of streams to restore cool shade for spawning trout. Decades of across-the-board suppression of forest fires, plus poor logging practices of the past, have created "dog hair" forests that are ecologically unnatural and threaten forests and neighboring communities with catastrophically intense fires. Restoring these lands to a healthy, naturally resilient condition will require removing large amounts of vegetation, and involve long-term stewardship—offering many decades of honorable, high-paying jobs for people in rural communities. An updated version of FDR's Civilian Conservation Corps can provide part of that labor—and offer meaningful work for tens of thousands of urban youth.

People across the American west are coming together in support of this vision. Loggers, timber companies, environmental leaders, and public resource agencies have ignored the demagogues who have tried to pit them against each other, and have found common ground in the effort to restore our public lands.[145] Public schools are joining the effort, with high school and college students getting academic credits for field work— taking water and soil samples to help monitor the results. These efforts need the support of all Americans. We can do this. And in the doing, we will rediscover our ties to the great American landscape, and the pride of caring for it well.

CLIMATE CHANGE

No problem we face is more grave than our excessive use of carbon-based energy, which is warming the planet. Unless we reverse course, we threaten life on earth as we know it.

We have the ability to change direction. Sustainable energy

sources and more efficient energy use—in everything from automobiles, to factories, to lightbulbs—will go a long way. With focused work we can tap into the limitless energy of hydrogen, which does not produce greenhouse gases. The only obstacles that have stood in our way have been lack of national will and the perversion of American democracy by special interests: Self-serving corporations have sought to protect profits at the expense of the earth's climate, supported in their greed by "free market" ideologues and corrupted politicians. We have allowed our energy-intensive way of life to jeopardize our own grandchildren. Making the transition will require investment—yes, it will cost us money. We have to stop complaining and step up to the plate:

▪ Using our global economic and technological preeminence, America must lead an international coalition in the battle against global warming. We will retrofit the American economy to assure that our use of energy is efficient, sustainable, and environmentally sound. And we will launch an international "Manhattan Project" to develop cost-effective non-carbon energy sources for the world.[146]

OTHER KEY CHALLENGES

The days are gone when we existed as an island, insulated from the rest of the world. Today, what happens in China, Argentina, Germany, or Syria affects us all. As the economic collapse of 2008 showed again, we are part of one world and we need to accept and act on that fundamental fact.

I interviewed Senator Mike Mansfield in the fall of 1999,

when he was 96. It was, I believe, the last interview of his life. He was a legendary figure who had worked in the Butte copper mines as a teenager, joined the navy at age fourteen, and served in World War I. He represented Montana in Congress for eleven years, and was a United States Senator from 1953 to 1977, rising to become Majority Leader. He introduced the 1964 Civil Rights Act, opposed the Vietnam War, and later served as ambassador to Japan under Presidents Carter and Reagan.

The interview was a distillation of decades of thinking, and deep experience. I asked him about a comment he'd made earlier, that "Our interdependence is a fact that we deny at our own peril."

And he said, "Events are forcing us to rethink our past thinking, our past sense of values, and to recognize that, in reality, we have to face up to . . . a new kind of life, highly technical, where we are integrated each with each other, where we are not islands unto ourselves, but parts of the whole. As such, we have to do what we can to make the world a better place for people to live in and to . . . become a partner with other countries and other peoples."

And this: "The essential ingredients of a healthy and secure society are good education and health, decent living conditions for all, a safe and clean environment, and the absence of poverty."

In 2003, the World Health Organization reported that *10.5 million children under five years of age were dying each year of easily preventable disease*, many as victims of drinking sewage-laden water.[147] As of 2009, 1.4 billion human beings lived in the worst sort of poverty, existing on less than $1.25 a day.[148] The moral imperative is clear, and so is practical necessity: Desperate people take desperate actions, and in the modern world they have access to very dangerous weapons.

At the 2000 UN Millennium Summit, world leaders committed themselves to eight targets that, when achieved, were to eliminate extreme poverty worldwide by 2015. All 192 members of the United Nations, including the United States, are in support. The goals included ending hunger, assuring universal primary education, achieving gender equality, empowering women, maternal and child health, combating HIV/AIDS and malaria, environmental sustainability, and developing a global partnership for economic development.

- America must take the leading role in supporting the Millennium timetable and action plan to end global poverty.

- We must emphasize approaches that have proven to be effective and achieve significant leverage, such as micro-loans to women to start small businesses and revitalize small-scale agriculture. Such support substantially raises living standards and results in higher school enrollment for children. A special effort is needed to supply inexpensive "low technology" clean water systems to those who need it; unlike centralized high-tech systems, they can be easily maintained. This action alone can save millions of lives.

By taking these steps, America will greatly reduce the number of children who die each year, enhance poor people's standard of living, and live up to our moral standards. And we will come to be seen again around the world as a nation committed to the elemental struggle for human justice.

As we work to recapture the American spirit we will make mistakes, we will stumble, we will have to reassess and adjust our approach. We will at times face doubt and fear, and will need courage to face them down. Demagogues will play on our fears, and try to deflect us from our course. But we will have a special strength on our side: We will have rekindled the Founding vision of America. We will have made the decision to stand alongside the women and men who went before, who in their time stepped forward and gave of themselves to improve their lives and the lives of their friends and neighbors, to carry forward the great Founding principles of freedom, responsibility, equality, and justice.

At the end of the day, at the end of our lives, we want to be able to honestly say that we lived our time well, we did our best to live up to the ideals in which we believed, and that in our short time on this earth, we left our world better for our children and grandchildren.

As a nation, as a people, and as individuals we have unprecedented choice. If we choose well, accepting the rights and responsibilities bequeathed us by the Founders, we will have stepped up to the challenge of our time. Then, each of us, at the end of our time, will be able to look in the mirror and say, "I gave my best."

In 1950 William Faulkner, perhaps the greatest of America's writers, won the Nobel Prize for literature. He lived in rural Mississippi and wrote about poor southerners, black and white, some who could read and some who could not, women and men who carried all the nobility and failings of humankind. He held nothing back, laying the human condition bare.

When Faulkner stood in Stockholm to accept the award, he said this: "Man is immortal, because he has a soul, a spirit capable of compassion and sacrifice and endurance."

Each of us has that soul, that spirit. And it will take them to succeed in what we must do if we are to fulfill our responsibility to the Founders, to those who came before us, and to the generations to come.

In April 1945, President Franklin Roosevelt wrote a speech to be delivered at the founding of the United Nations in San Francisco. Exhausted by leading America through the Great Depression, and to victory in the war against fascism, he died before he could deliver it.

He wrote:

> Today we are faced with the fact that, if civilization is to survive, we must cultivate the science of human relationships—the ability of all peoples, of all kinds, to live together and work together in the same world, at peace. . . .
>
> The only limit to our realization of tomorrow will be our doubts of today. Let us move forward with strong and active faith.

We have work to do. And we can do it.

ACKNOWLEDGMENTS

I have many people to thank:

The many Montanans who responded so positively to the "American Values" speech I gave across the states. Their enthusiasm inspired me, and led to the decision to put my thoughts into a book.

My brother Steve's early enthusiasm for the idea encouraged me to sit down to write.

Friends generously helped me improve the manuscript at various stages, offering serious comments, criticisms, and suggestions: Don Albini, Jock Anderson, Sue Bartlett, Clay Clement, Kim Clement, Katherine Dayton, Gene Fenderson, Chris King, Stan Meyer, Phil Nemir, George Royle, David Sirota, and Bill Weeks.

My wife, Sandra Dal Poggetto offered strong, consistent encouragement and stoically endured many weekends and nights of work, as well as strained author's moods. My son, Dylan, during visits home from college, was always interested and supportive.

During these hard times in publishing, literary agent Jennifer Lyons took on the project, stayed with it, found it a good home.

Editor Crystal Yakacki, though young in years, is an editor of the old, well-fashioned school. She cares about her books, and pushed me to improve it.

And the family Lab, Tess. I had done the typing for her book, *Training People: How to Bring Out the Best in Your Human.* She generously returned the favor, unfailingly pulling me away from the troubles, flaws, and foibles of us humans to the warm, sane world of the Dog.

Finally, my parents, who encouraged me to look, helped enable me to see, and believed in a future worthy of mankind.

POLITICAL DEFINITIONS

This book is about the priorities and choices facing our country, choices that will be determined by personal values and political philosophy. Political "labels" have different meanings to different people, and their definitions change with time. My grandfather, for example, was a Republican industrialist. He proudly considered himself "conservative." He would be appalled to find that word applied to support "free market" policies that encourage citizens to buy consumer goods, even food, on credit. To him, credit cards promoted shallow materialism and financial irresponsibility at the expense of bedrock conservative values, including paying as you go, personal thrift, and the responsibility to save for future needs.[149] Gramps' definition of conservatism was broadly shared at that time. In our fast and loose consumer-driven economy, many who today claim the "conservative" label would consider his ideas hopelessly out of date.

Additionally, almost all of us have personal opinions that include elements of different political philosophies. In that sense, labels do an injustice to the complexity of our views. In my own case, I consider myself a "progressive." However, important elements of my personal values are old-fashioned "conservative."

All such labels are subject to legitimate disagreement—each reader of this book will have her or his own. Given the variation in political definitions, it is important to be clear about their use in this book. Following are my definitions of the political categories I use.

CONSERVATIVE

A person who follows the philosophy that emphasizes the importance of respect for established customs and institutions, for social order, continuity with tradition, property rights, hard work, self-reliance, and personal responsibility. Regards government and taxation skeptically, especially where it constrains business or property. Supports strong government in the areas of the military, police, and policies that favor business. Is skeptical that social circumstances such as poverty impact personal behavior, or that violence/crime can be addressed by publicly funded efforts to reduce poverty, assure education, etc. Tends to the view that society's hierarchy of wealth, position, and power reflects merit, rather than mere good fortune: Those at the top have earned their position, while those at the bottom have earned theirs. Hence, opposes tax/spending policies that distribute wealth downward, and supports those that distribute wealth upward.

FREE MARKET "CONSERVATIVE"

Believes the "invisible hand" of markets is the best tool for creating wealth and achieving economic growth, which eventually benefits all segments of society. Sees government taxation and regulation of business and private property as inefficient, counter-productive, and/or a denial of personal and economic freedom. While traditional conservatives place high value on social tradition and stability, free market advocates understand that market forces are among the most potent causes of erosion of traditional social values—and support giving them a free hand to do so. Hence, I place quotation marks: Free market "conservative." Like traditional conservatives, favors tax/spending policies that favor business, entrepreneurial individuals, and the wealthy—the "job-producing" sections of society.

LIBERTARIAN

Fundamentally skeptical of government laws, taxation, and regulation, believing these are infringements on personal liberty. Some libertarians oppose all concentrated power—private and public—as oppressive of individual freedom. Others, both "pro-corporate" and "free market" libertarians, consider corporate economic power as the logical and appropriate result of economic liberty, even when that power infringes on individual rights.

LIBERAL

Places high value on the intrinsic worth of the individual, personal human rights, and the potential of human beings and society to enhance tolerance and reduce violence over time. Feels that a reasonable distribution of wealth and equal opportunity is essential to fulfillment of people's rights and potential, and that the personal values and behavior of people are seriously impacted by their social circumstances. Is concerned about the negative impacts of unregulated market forces on people and the environment, and supports government intervention to mitigate these through taxation, incentives, and regulation. Tends to support such wealth redistribution programs as Social Security and Medicare, taxation/spending for anti-poverty efforts and public education, and care for the disabled. Tends to the view that sexual preference is a legitimate adult choice, that a woman has the right to terminate pregnancy, favors clear separation of church and state, and religious tolerance.

PROGRESSIVE

Shares liberals' concerns for fairness/social justice and the negative impacts of unregulated market forces on people, the environment, and society as a whole. Shares conservatives' belief in hard work and individual responsibility, but defines that responsibility as extending beyond self and family to the community and larger world. Believes that a consumer-driven economy and culture fundamentally misdirects social values toward a shallow materialism, undermining the ability of individuals and the community to focus on important public issues. Strongly concerned about "anti-democratic" impacts of concentrated corporate economic and political power, and supports strong government policies to reduce or decentralize that power.

REACTIONARY

Holds extreme conservative or libertarian views. Believes that rights of property and commerce are superior to all other human rights. Strongly opposes legislation regulating business practices and use of property in ways that reduce profitability. Is philosophically opposed to many twentieth-century reforms that broadened distribution of economic wealth, such as progressive income tax, minimum wage, unemployment insurance, food stamps, Social Security, and Medicare. Considers such efforts to be stealing wealth from those who earned it to give to those who have not. Denies that government has a legitimate role in encouraging ethnic or gender equality, or conservation of the environment. Believes "survival of the fittest" appropriately applies to human society. In the text, I refer to those who advocate such views as the far or extreme Right.

These "philosophies" have played, and still play, a major role in our nation's history—both the dark and the light. The application of one or another through public policy will lead to profoundly different consequences for our children and grandchildren, our communities and our nation.

NOTES

1. Chris Isidore, "Recession Job Losses: Worse Than First Thought," *CNN-Money.com*, October 12, 2010.
2. Associated Press, "U.S. Home Foreclosure Notices Hit 274,000 in January," CBC News, February 12, 2010.
3. Bob Herbert, "The Horror Show," *New York Times*, August 10, 2010.
4. 2010 Census Bureau report. *New York Times*, September 17, 2010.
5. Bill Moyers, "Moyers & FDR," *Nation*, November 21, 2007. In total, almost one out of three Americans is low income.
6. Zhu Xiao Di, *Growing Wealth, Inequality, and Housing in the United States* (Cambridge: Joint Center for Housing Studies, Harvard University, 2007); Robert B. Reich, "How to End the Great Recession," *New York Times*, September 2, 2010. In the late 1970s, the top 1 percent received only 9 percent of total income. Meanwhile, the median male worker earns less today, adjusted for inflation, than thirty years ago, and works one hundred hours more per year.
7. Nelson D. Schwarz and Louise Story, "Pay of Hedge Fund Managers Roared Back Last Year," *New York Times*, March 31, 2010.
8. Amanda Gardner, "Many Americans Don't Even Know They're Fat," *Bloomberg Businessweek*, September 2, 2010.
9. Timothy S. Grall, *Custodial Mothers and Fathers and Their Child Support: 2007* (Washington: US Census Bureau, 2009).
10. Roy Walmsley, *World Prison Population List* (London: International Centre for Prison Studies, 2009). In 2002, our rate of incarceration per 100,000 people was five times that of Britain, and about seven times that of France, Germany, and Canada.
11. World Bank, 2010 World Development Indicators (Washington: The World Bank, 2010).

12. Harvey Cox, "The Market as God," *Atlantic Monthly*, March 1999. Written by Professor Harvey Cox of Harvard University's Divinity School, the article describes how pro-market ideology and language present market forces as wise, omnipotent, and God-like.

13. Abraham Lincoln, "First Debate with Stephen A. Douglas at Ottawa" (speech, Ottawa, Illinois, August 21, 1858). Emphasis is Lincoln's.

14. The contradiction between American values and the reality of slavery in part was the result of racism—the dehumanizing of other people in order to "justify" oppression. The sanctity of "property rights" was also a major factor—the "right" to own human beings and to buy and sell them in the "free market." Any proposal to end slavery was opposed as an "attack on private property rights."

15. James Buchan, *The Authentic Adam Smith* (New York: W.W. Norton, 2006), 3.

16. John Adams to James Sullivan, May 26, 1776. In this letter, Adams wrote, "Harrington has shown that power always follows property. This I believe to be as infallible a maxim in politics, as that action and reaction are equal is in mechanics. Nay, I believe we may advance one step farther, and affirm that the balance of power in a society accompanies the balance of property in land. The only possible way, then, of preserving the balance of power on the side of equal liberty and public virtue is to make the acquisition of land easy to every member of society; to make a division of the land into small quantities, so that the multitude may be possessed of landed estates."

17. Alexander H. Stephens, "Cornerstone Speech" (speech, Savannah, Georgia, March 21, 1861). The doctrine of "states' rights" was the rallying cry of slave owners, just as it would be for segregationists and many of today's extreme free market/libertarian "conservatives." The resurgent Confederacy heritage movement, also using "states' rights," attempts to place the South and Jefferson Davis on equal moral ground with Lincoln and the Union. But they are careful not to quote Stephens 'corner-stone' speech.

18. Ben Rooney and Kenneth Musante, "Oil Touches Record But Ends Lower," *CNNMoney.com*, June 30, 2008.

19. John Adams, *A Constitution or Form of Government for the Commonwealth of Massachusetts* (1779).

20. Between 1850 and 1871, railroads were given a total of 175 million acres of federal land by Congress, or more than 10 percent of the nation.

21. Abraham Lincoln, "On Labor and Capital" (A message to the US Congress, December 3, 1861).

22. Steven Mufson, "Massey Energy has Litany of Critics, Violations," *Washington Post*, April 6, 2010.

23. Stephen Ambrose, *Supreme Commander* (New York: Doubleday, 1970), 322.

24. Peter S. Goodman, "Economy Shrinks With Consumers Leading the Way," *New York Times*, October 30, 2010.

25. Allan Brandt, *The Cigarette Century* (New York: Basic Books, 2008).

26. David M. Burns, Lora Lee, Larry Z. Shen, Elizabeth Gilpin, H. Dennis Tolley, Jerry Vaughn, and Thomas G. Shanks, "Cigarette Smoking Behavior in the United States," Tobacco Control Monograph Series.

27. "Facts About Smoking," Santa Clara County Public Health Department.

28. Louise Story, "Anywhere the Eye Can See, It's Likely to See an Ad," *New York Times*, January 15, 2007.

29. The text of the 1934 Communications Act that establishes these rules mentions "the public interest" more than one hundred times.

30. Debra J Holt, Pauline M. Ippolito, Debra M. Desrochers, and Christopher R. Kelley. *Children's Exposure to TV Advertising in 1977 and 2004: Information for the Obesity Debate* (Federal Trade Commission Bureau of Economics, 2007). Between the ages of two to eleven, children see more than 25,000 advertisements on TV alone. Until age eight, children do not understand that advertising is intended to persuade them.

31. "Children and Television," The Museum of Broadcast Communications, accessed October 12, 2010, http://www.museum.tv/eotvsection.php?entrycode=childrenand.

32. Christine Lagorio, "Resources: Marketing to Kids: Statistics, Reports and Books About How Companies Target Toddlers to Teens," CBS News, May 17, 2007. The $17 billion figure is more than double what was spent in 1992.

33. Bootie Cosgrove-Mather, "Ads for High-Fat Foods Permeate Toddler TV," Associated Press, October 2, 2006. This AP story reported findings of a study conducted by Cleveland's Rainbow Babies and Children's Hospital and stated, "Fast food companies dominated sponsor messages during program for toddlers . . . making up 82 percent of sponsor messages on PBS preschool programming and 36 percent of messages on Disney's toddler block of shows."

34. Amanda Gardner, "Many Americans Don't Even Know They're Fat," *Bloomberg Businessweek*, September 2, 2010.

35. James Dao, "Making Soldiers Fit to Fight, Without the Situps," *New York Times*, August 30, 2010. The obesity epidemic is even affecting national security. In 2010, a group of retired admirals and generals issued a report, "Too Fat to Fight," which stated, "Between 1995 and 2008, the proportion of potential recruits who failed their physicals each year because they were over-weight rose nearly 70 percent." The percentage of male recruits who failed physicals increased from 4 percent in 2000 to more than 20 percent in 2006.

36. Melanie Warner, "Under Pressure, Food Producers Shift to Healthier Products," *New York Times*, December 16, 2005.

37. Hibah Yousuf, "Personal Bankruptcies Surge 9%," *CNNMoney.com*, November 4, 2009; Chris Isidore, "Recession Job Losses: Worse Than First Thought," *CNNMoney.com*, October 12, 2010.

38. Emphasis added.

39. Thomas Jefferson, from the president to Messrs. Dodge, Robbins, and Nelson, January 1, 1802

40. There are many types of corporations. For simplicity, I use the word to mean large, publicly held corporations traded on stock exchanges.

41. It is important to recognize that some highly successful corporations resist these pressures. Costco pays its employees far above industry standards, and has an extraordinary company policy to enforce *low* profit margins. Starbucks provides health insurance to all employees, including those who work part time. The experience of such companies is important to inform public policy changes to encourage such behavior.

42. In an ironic twist, this lack of human conscience results in the inability to prosecute corporations for certain acts that would be criminal if done by a human being. In the words of Sir Edward Coke, "[Corporations] cannot commit treason, nor be outlawed nor excommunicated, for they have no souls."

43. The influence is now creeping into the election of judges. Example: In 2004, after Massey Coal lost a $50 million fraud verdict, Massey's owner donated $3 million to the campaign of Brent Benjamin, a candidate for the West Virginia Court of Appeals. Elected to the court, Benjamin was the swing vote overturning the verdict. On a 5–4 vote, the US Supreme Court reversed that ruling.

44. "Ayn Rand—Conservatives," YouTube video, 4:51, posted by "Scoforever," October 13, 2009, http://www.youtube.com/watch?v=BRzmAwLmXiE.

45. Jennifer Brooks, *Goddess of the Market: Ayn Rand and the American Right* (New York: Oxford University Press, 2009), 105–106. Brooks writes: "She believed that it was altruism itself that had brought Europe to the brink of destruction. . . . Rand summarized her thoughts: '19th Century Liberalism made the mistake of associating liberty, rights of man, etc. with the idea of 'fighting for the people,' 'for the downtrodden,' 'for the poor,' etc. They made it an altruistic movement. But altruism is collectivism.'" Later, Rand wrote, "Independence of man from men is the Life Principle. Dependence of man upon men is the Death Principle." While we all have elements of our personal lives that are inconsistent with our ideals, it seems particularly ironic that Rand, the absolutist advocate of personal freedom, had her husband wear a bell on his shoe so she could keep track of him (Brooks 108).

46. Ibid., 206.

47. Mark Leibovich, "Being Glenn Beck," *New York Times Magazine*, October 3, 2010. Sean Hannity and Rush Limbaugh also echo Rand, and the Tea Party's core principles closely mirror her absolutist support for "economic liberty" and opposition to public "welfare." So do the views of extremist libertarian David Koch, the oil magnate billionaire who funds numerous ultra-Right causes and think tanks. In August 2010, FreedomWorks (a spin-off of a Koch-funded group) held voter outreach training sessions for Tea Party activists who had come to Washington DC for the Glenn Beck/Sarah Palin rally at the Lincoln Memorial. Hanging in FreedomWorks' office was a portrait of Ayn Rand.

48. Brooks, *Goddess of the Market*, 204.

49. Greenspan collaborated with Rand on *Capitalism: The Unknown Ideal.*

50. Erik Eckholm, "Recession Raises Poverty Rate to a 15-Year High," 2010 Census Bureau Report, *New York Times*, September 17, 2010. The Bush II tax cuts were supposed to help average Americans. But between 1999 and 2009, their median income declined by 5 percent.

51. During the Bush II years, Norquist emerged as one of the most influential Republicans in Washington.

52. David Kocieniewski, "A Wake Up Call for the Middle Class," *New York, Times*, November 13, 2010.

53. Anthony Crupi, "Report: Ad Growth Flat in 2010," *Brandweek*, January 19, 2010.

54. The Fairness Doctrine was revoked by a vote of FCC Commissioners in 1987.

55. Edward R. Murrow, "Radio-Television News Directors Association and Foundation Speech" (speech, Chicago, IL, October 15, 1958).

56. Ben H. Bagdikian, *The New Media Monopoly* (New York: Beacon Press, 2004).

57. Chris Peck, editor, "The Commercial Appeal" (speech, Wheeler Center Roundtable, Missoula, Montana, 2009). Between 2007 and the end of 2009, 36,000 journalism jobs, including 25,000 from print publications, were eliminated in America as news enterprises tried to cut costs and maintain profits.

58. Fox ignores news about continuing ethnic discrimination in America, but shamelessly promoted the doctored video of Shirley Sherrod, a Department of Agriculture official, claiming she was a black racist. When the truth was revealed they admitted no wrong, then blamed the Obama Administration for firing her.

59. Encyclopædia Britannica, "Nazi Party," *Encyclopædia Britannica's Reflections on the Holocaust*, accessed October 12, 2010, http://www.britannica.com/holocaust/article-9055111.

60. Many on the Right would like to see all public land privatized. Some years ago I talked with the co-founder of a Montana-based "free market" think tank. An economist, he had written extensively about the superiority of private over public land, and had proposed federal lands be sold to the private sector. When I asked why the think tank did not publicly identify itself with this idea, he said that it simply was not politically feasible. Of course, he still thought it was a good idea.

61. At times during the Iraq War, private, for-profit contractors paid by the US government outnumbered our troops. Even the interrogation of prisoners was contracted out—with disastrous results.

62. Andrew Coates MD, "Two-Thirds of Americans Support Medicare-for-All," *Physicians for a National Health Program Official Blog*, December 9, 2009, http://pnhp.org/blog/2009/12/09/two-thirds-support-3/. National polls in 2009 showed that a majority of Americans supported this approach to health insurance.

63. Pew Research Center for the People & the Press, "Internet Overtakes Newspapers As News Outlets," *Pew Research Center Publications*, December 23, 2008.

64. A.C. Hanson, *TV-Free America Report, 2007*, http://www.csun.edu/science/health/docs/tv&health.html; A.C. Hanson, *Big World, Small Screen* (Lincoln: University of Nebraska Press, 1992).

65. American Academy of Child & Adolescent Psychiatry, "Children And Watching TV," *Facts for Families* No. 54, (American Academy of Child & Adolescent Psychiatry, 2001).

66. Theodore Roosevelt, "The New Nationalism" (speech, Osawatomie, TX, September 1910). In 1779, John Adams expressed much the same view in language he wrote for the constitution of the new Commonwealth of Massachusetts: "No man, nor corporation or association of men have any other title to obtain advantages or particular and exclusive privileges distinct from those of the community, than what arises from the consideration of services rendered to the public . . ."

67. Media consolidation has greatly eroded local news coverage on radio, TV, and newspapers, undercutting the ability of citizens to be knowledgeable and engaged in their communities.

68. Debates of the Federal Convention, June 18, 1787. Stripped of rhetoric, the American Right adheres to Hamilton's view. But they want to take it one step further: permanent *dominance* of government by "the first class."

69. *US Census 2010*, http://www.census.gov/Press-Release/www/releases/archives/voting/012234.html.

70. Charles M. Blow, "What's Dumb, Really?" *New York Times*, October 1, 2010.

71. This appearance was only partially true: The Louisiana Purchase, Union victory in the Civil War, building of the Erie Canal, roads, trans-continental railroad, the Homestead Act, and the establishment of Land Grant Colleges across the nation were just some of the government actions that were essential to the country's development.

72. Separate from the moral hollowness of that goal, it lays the foundation for disillusionment. Only a minority of Americans are rich. The goal of becoming wealthy is thus out of reach for the large majority of people, setting them up for inevitable "failure," and disillusionment with themselves, and their country.

73. Anne D. Neal and Jeremy L. Martin, *Losing America's Memory: Historical Illiteracy in the 21st Century* (Washington: American Council of Trustees and Alumni, 2000).

74. Michael K. Block and Robert J. Franciosi, *What do College Graduates Know? A Survey of Arizona Universities* (2002).

75. Data from Social Security Administration, Trustee Report (Washington DC, US Government, 2007).

76. Social Security deducts 6.2 percent from the employee's gross pay, with the employer adding an equal match of his own. The tax is levied against the first $106,800 of an employee's salary; above that amount, there is no tax. Medicare receives similar support—2.9 percent for employee and employer.

77. "Volunteering in the U.S.," *Volunteering in America*, accessed October 12, 2010, http://www.volunteeringinamerica.gov/national.

78. Glenn Beck labels the Progressive movement as a totalitarian "cancer," in lock step with communism and fascism. Teddy Roosevelt would laugh.

79. Center for Responsive Politics, "Fundraising Over Time," *Open Secrets*, accessed October 12, 2010, http://www.crp.org.

80. "Ron Brown Scholar Program," accessed October 15, 2010, http://www.ron-brown.org/home.aspx; Sandy Bergo, "A Wealth of Advice: Nearly $2 Billion Flowed Through Consultants in 2003-2004 Federal Elections," The Center for Public Integrity, September 26, 2006. In 2004, the average cost of winning a Senate seat was $7 million; a House seat $1 million. According to numbers released by the Federal Election Commission, in the 2009-10 election cycle, $354 million was spent on thirty-four Senate races—$10.4 million per seat.

81. Gary Jason, "Orange Grove: Obama's Surge in Government Jobs," *Orange County Register*, February 22, 2010.

82. Ibid.

83. The unemployment problem in China includes 150 million surplus rural laborers.

84. Parija Kavilanz, "Wal-Mart Suffers Sales Decline in Key Quarter," *CNN-Money.com*, February 18, 2010.

85. Michael J. Hicks, "Does Wal-Mart Cause an Increase in Anti-Poverty Program Expenditures?" *New York Times*, August 26, 2010. More than one million present and former women Wal-Mart employees filed a class action lawsuit alleging discrimination in pay and promotions. Betty Dukes is one. After working for Wal-Mart for nine years, her salary was $8.44 an hour.

86. Theodore Roosevelt, "The New Nationalism."

87. Postage is a major expense in congressional campaigns. The cost to the public of free election mailings would be negligible, since the postal system's operating costs are already in place.

88. The internet has emerged as an effective source of increasing grassroots political participation and the raising of tens of millions of dollars in small contributions. For decades, millions of Americans—scattered across the entire nation—have cared about our democracy, but lacked an easy way to contribute to candidates of their choice. Web-based fundraising has changed that, and federal law needs to assure continued free internet access for such activity.

89. The *Journal*'s comment highlights a key question: Should we expect the conduct of business to reflect moral values held by society? Like Ayn Rand, free market libertarians and the extreme Right promote greed and self-focused pursuit of wealth as virtues. Why do they try to convince the American people of this? Because they know that if the community demands that the conduct of business reflect *true* moral values, increased regulation will follow.

90. David L. Lewis, *The Public Image of Henry Ford* (Detroit: Wayne State University Press, 1976), 99; Neil Baldwin, *Henry Ford and the Jews* (New York: Public Affairs, 2001), 36–39.

91. President Calvin Coolidge, "Address to the American Society of Newspaper Editors" (speech, Washington DC, January 25, 1925).

92. Albert E. Kahn, *High Treason* (New York: Lear Publishers, 1950), 104.

93. "Co-determination," *Wikipedia: The Free Encyclopedia*, accessed October 12, 2010, http://en.wikipedia.org/wiki/Co-determination.

94. The conversation took place before Racicot became an early backer of George W. Bush's presidential bid; before he moved to Washington DC, to become a partner in the high-powered lobbying law firm of Bracewell and Patterson, taking Enron as a major client.

95. Fareed Zakaria, "To Deal With the Deficit, Let the Tax Cuts Expire," *Washington Post*, August 2, 2010.

96. Nelson Mandela, *Long Walk to Freedom: The Autobiography of Nelson Mandela* (New York: Back Bay Books, 1995), 175. Interestingly, in 1955 in South Africa, 27 percent of population owned 87 percent of the land. Seventy-three percent (blacks) owned 13 percent.

97. The question is not new in our time. In 1785, Thomas Jefferson criticized the intense concentration of wealth and property in France, arguing that it sharply hindered economic development. He advocated changes in inheritance laws and a progressive property tax, with higher rates for larger holdings.

98. Edward. N. Wolff, "Recent Trends in the Size Distribution of Household Wealth," *Journal of Economic Perspectives* 12 no. 3 (1998). In 1997, Bill Gates' net worth was roughly equal to that of 40 million American households; L. Kroll and A. Fass, "The World's Richest People," *Forbes*, March 3, 2007. In 2006, the world's billionaires were worth more than twice as much as the 2.4 billion people living in the poorest countries—37 percent of humanity.

99. Theodore Roosevelt, "The New Nationalism."

100. Glenn Beck, *Glenn Beck's Common Sense: The Case Against Out-of-Control Government, Inspired by Thomas Paine* (New York: Threshold Editions, June 2009). The extreme Right's attack on "high taxes" and for "limited government" is in reality an attack on precisely those public institutions that increase equality of opportunity. Glenn Beck exemplifies this mindset when he attacks public commitment to "fairness" and a "safety net" and cheers, "the causes of liberty, capitalism, inventiveness and the progressive principle of natural selection."

101. Smith would scoff at the claim. For example, he argued that for a business, success meant more capital, which was invested to expand the business with increased local labor, which raised wages for workers. Today, global capital moves anywhere it wishes to find cheap labor, driving down wages for similar jobs in developed countries, or simply wiping them out.

102. Adam Smith, *Wealth of Nations, Book Five: Of the Revenue of the Sovereign or Commonwealth* (1776).

103. Theodore Roosevelt, "The New Nationalism." T. R. thought estates should be taxed so that major wealth was not passed on to those who had not earned it through the competition of the marketplace.

104. *The Tax Adviser*, December, 1997.

105. G. William Domhoff, "Wealth, Income and Power," Who Rules America?, University of California at Santa Cruz, September 2005, accessed October 15, 2010,

http://sociology.ucsc.edu/whorulesamerica/power/wealth.html. In 2007, 75 percent of the income of the top 400 income earners in America came from capital
gains and dividends.

106. Internal Revenue Service, *Corporation Income Tax Brackets and Rates, 1909-2002*,
http://www.irs.gov/pub/irs-soi/02corate.pdf.

107. The 2008 presidential campaign debate about "wealth redistribution" reflects this
fundamental bias. According to John McCain and his supporters, any attempt to
shift more income to lower and middle class Americans amounted to "socialism."
But the 2008 Bush Administration TARP bailouts—wealth redistribution to
major corporations of hundreds of billions of dollars—did not.

108. "Our Work," American Farmland Trust, accessed October 15, 2010,
http://www.farmland.org/programs/default.asp.

109. Sue Stock, "Shoppers Still Choosing Organic Food," *Modesto Bee*, June 21, 2008.

110. The southern states insisted that slaves—who were considered to be property with
no rights whatsoever—be counted in determining the number of seats they would
receive in Congress. In one of the most depraved "compromises" in history, it was
agreed that five slaves would be counted as three human beings.

111. Theodore Roosevelt, "The New Nationalism."

112. In 2007, I interviewed the Republican Speaker of the Montana House of Representatives Scott Sales. Mr. Sales became wealthy through stock appreciation in a
start-up software company, and, at the time, earned his living as a private investor.
He described himself as, "an outspoken conservative." During the interview, I
asked him if he felt it was appropriate for government to redistribute wealth, and
he responded, "Absolutely not." "Then as a matter of principle," I said, "You must
oppose Social Security, since it is the largest wealth redistribution program in the
nation's history." He tried to avoid answering, saying that the system needed to be
made solvent. But when I pressed him he finally admitted, "Well, I wouldn't have
set it up that way." Indeed.

113. Led by England's Prime Minister Neville Chamberlain, and supported in the
United States by prominent Americans like Henry Ford, Charles Lindberg, and
Senator Burton K. Wheeler, isolationists and conservatives prevented the formation of an anti-fascist coalition to confront Hitler when he was still weak. Major
American corporations invested in the German and Italian economies, and built
factories there that would be used to produce tanks and planes that killed Americans. In 1938, at the order of Hitler, Henry Ford was awarded the Grand Cross
of the German Eagle—the highest honor Nazi Germany could bestow on for-
eigners. Lindberg received the same award later the same year. By delaying the
anti-fascist alliance and enabling Hitler to gather strength through the conquest
of Austria, Czechoslovakia, France, and the Netherlands, the conservative
appeasers caused the deaths of millions of human beings.

114. In 1997, the Montana Supreme Court unanimously overturned the law, saying it
violated the state constitution's right to privacy. In 2010, the platform of the Montana Republican Party called for re-instatement of homosexuality as a crime.

115. Eight nations abstained, including the Soviet bloc, Yugoslavia, South Africa and Saudi Arabia.

116. Zhu Xiao Di, *Growing Wealth, Inequality, and Housing in the United States* (Cambridge: Joint Center for Housing Studies, Harvard University, 2007).

117. Ibid.

118. Department of the Treasury Report, November 3, 2008. In 2010, long-term capital gains taxes ranged from zero to 15 percent, depending on the category of investment and the owner's income. US Treasury Department annual revenues from 2000 to 2006 from this tax averaged $75 billion.

119. Interestingly, this "push the money to the top" advocacy became increasingly blatant after the global collapse of Marxist socialism. During the Cold War, the Russians criticized our nation as being controlled by millionaires, and ignoring poverty. In the international battle for public opinion, it did not serve our interests to argue that the people and corporations at the top were our most productive citizens, the engines of prosperity, and fully deserving of their immense wealth. Instead, we argued that the American and western European capitalist economies were outperforming the socialist ones *and creating a higher standard of living for everyday people.*

   With the global socialist challenge a thing of the past, the economic elite's argument shifted: Send more of the nation's wealth to the top, and the "free market" will insure that an appropriate amount will "trickle down" to the rest. And any direct attempt to increase income levels for everyday people is "socialism."

120. Thomas Jefferson to Edward Carrington, 1787.

121. Joseph P. Lasch, *Eleanor and Franklin* (Old Saybrook: Konecky and Konecky, 1971), 27.

122. Emphasis in original.

123. Ron Haskins, "Wealth and Economic Mobility," Economic Mobility Project, 2007.

124. Business advocates of the time applauded this type of government intervention in the economy.

125. Jon Gertner, "What is a Living Wage?," *New York Times*, January 15, 2006. Massachusetts enacted minimum wage legislation in 1912. Congress did the same in 1938, establishing a federal minimum of 25 cents an hour.

126. Carmen DeNavas-Wait, Bernadette D. Proctor, and Cheryl Hill Lee, *Income, Poverty, and Health Insurance Coverage in the United States: 2005* (Washington: US Census Bureau, 2006); J.S. Hacker, *The Great Risk Shift: The New Insecurity and the Decline of the American Dream* (New York: Oxford University Press, 2006).

127. US Department of Health & Human Services, *Extension of the 2009 Poverty Guidelines Until at Least May 31, 2010.*

128. Department of Labor, *Characteristics of Minimum Wage Workers* (2009).

129. John M. Abowd, *Minimum Wages and Youth Employment in France and the United States* (Ithaca: Cornell University, May 1997).

130. Montana Department of Public Health and Human Services website.

131. "Supplemental Nutrition Assistance Program," United States Department of Agriculture, accessed October 12, 2010, http://www.fns.usda.gov/snap/faqs.htm#9.

132. Erik Eckholm, "Recession Raises Poverty Rate to a 15-Year High," *New York Times*, September 16, 2010; Sarah Fass and Nancy K. Cauthen, "Who Are America's Poor Children?," National Center for Children in Poverty, November 2007, http://www.nccp.org/publications/pub_787.html. In 2007, 13 million children lived below the official poverty line and 39 million American children were low-income (families earning less than $42,000 for a family of four).

133. When I served as a member of the California Board of Corrections in the early 1980s, the state's prison population was 35,000—the highest in the nation. Twenty-five years later, it was 120,000.

134. "CBS Poll: 81% Say U.S. On the Wrong Track," CBS News, April 3, 2008.

135. Martin Luther King, Jr., "When Silence is Betrayal" (speech, Riverside Church, New York City, April 4, 1967).

136. "Born of Controversy: The GI Bill of Rights," GI Bill History, United States Department of Veteran Affairs, accessed October 12, 2010, http://www.gibill.va .gov/gi_bill_info/history.htm.

137. Paul Attwell and David Lavin, *Passing the Torch: Does Higher Education for the Disadvantaged Pay Off Across the Generations?* (New York: Russell Sage Foundation Publications, 2007).

138. Trip Gabriel, "Academic Standing of Black Males is Found to be Bleaker than Expected," *New York Times*, November 9, 2010. The article summarizes the 2010 report, "A Call for Change," released by the Council of Greater City Schools.

139. "The Achievement Gap," *Education Week*, September 10, 2004.

140. Tamar Lewin, "Once a Leader, U.S. Lags in College Degrees," *New York Times*, July 23, 2010.

141. Steve Sternberg, "18,000 Deaths Blamed on Lack of Insurance," *USA Today*, May 22, 2002; Nicholas D. Kristof, "A Short American Life," *New York Times*, May 21, 2007. An American woman is 50 percent more likely to die in childbirth than one in Europe. If our infant mortality rate was that of Germany, France, and Italy, we would save 12,000 children a year.

142. John Fritze, "Medical Expenses Have 'Very Steep Rate of Growth,'" *USA Today*, February 4, 2010.

143. Duff Wilson, "Medical Industry Ties Often Undisclosed in Journals," *New York Times*, September 13, 2010. A largely hidden issue is profit-driven medicine, where incentives encourage treatment based on personal profit instead of patient care. In 2009, I interviewed Dr. Tom Weiner, head oncologist at Helena, Montana's St. Peter's Hospital. He said that it is common for oncologists to buy cancer drugs wholesale, and charge retail prices to their patients. He believed a majority use a computerized "reimbursement calculator," which analyzes the patient's cancer, the range of appropriate drugs, *and the doctor's profit margin for each*. He himself did not do that. Another example is doctors who receive large "consulting fees" from

drug and medical device companies, and then promote those products to patients and other doctors. A study of five medical device companies showed payments of about $250 million to consultants, including royalties on sales. Of that amount, $141 million went to forty-one doctors who earned up to $8.8 million each.

144. Denise Grady, "Obesity Rates Keep Rising, Troubling Health Officials," *New York Times*, August 3, 2010. In 2010, obesity rates reached 30 percent or more in nine states, up from three states in 2007. 72.5 million Americans are obese, more than one out of four.

145. *Restoring Montana's National Forest Lands* (Missoula: Montana Forest Restoration Working Group, 2007). This report details principles for ecologically grounded and economically viable principles for restoration of our national forests. In 2010, the Secretary of Agriculture awarded $10 million to ten pioneering national forest projects designed to achieve restoration on a landscape scale. See http://www.montanarestoration.org.

146. The World War II Manhattan Project was the crash effort by the United States to develop the atomic bomb before the Nazis were successful in doing so.

147. "Surviving the First Five Years of Life," World Health Organization, accessed October 12, 2010, http://www.who.int/whr/2003/chapter1/en/index2.html.

148. "World Bank Revises Poverty Estimates," Bank Information Center, August 28, 2010, http://www.bicusa.org/en/Article.3887.aspx.

149. David Brooks, "The Next Culture War," *New York Times*, September 28, 2010. In 1960, American's personal debt amounted to 55 percent of national income. In 2007, it equaled 133 percent of national income.

INDEX

abortion, 149–50
  as crime, 59
Adams, John, 85–86, 129, 206n66
  on body politic, 34–35
  on power, 27
  to his son, 129
  to Sullivan, 202n16
advertising, 41–42. *See also* American
  Values Advertising Fund; network
  advertising
  cartoon heroes and, 44
  children, aimed at, 43–49, 203n30
  cigarettes, 42
  engineered individual choice, 42
  failure of representative government
    in, 48–49
  public interest and, 84
  public service, 83–84
Alighieri, Dante, 87
Ambrose, Stephen, 35
American Civil Liberties Union, 69
Americans for Tax Reforms, 58
American spirit, 191–92
Americans with Disabilities, 150
American values, 14, 94. *See also specific
  values*
American Values Advertising Fund, 82–
  83, 86, 179–80
"American Values for Our Time," 78–82
Anaconda Mining and Smelter Company, 113
animal domestication, 26
anti-discrimination laws, 58
anti-immigrant politics, 31
anti-pollution laws, 114
aristocracy, 27
Army, recruitment slogan, 37–40
Arsenal of Democracy, 146

Articles of Confederation, "states'
  rights" structure of, 33
atomic power, 29

bailout
  Bush Administration, 119, 209n107
  Mexican banks, 30
  taxpayer-funded, 48
bankruptcy protection, 59
banks
  deregulation of, 58
  failure of representative government
    in, 48–49
  Mexican, 30
Beck, Glenn, 70, 141, 208n100
  label for progressive movement,
    206n78
  Obama Administration and, 68–69
  Rand, references to, 56
Belt, Montana, 116
Benedict (Pope), 125–27
Benjamin, Brent, 204n43
Bertelsmann, 68
Biden, Joe, 89
Big Four, 35–36
Bill of Rights, 24
  human rights in, 152
bitching, alternative to, 23
Blair, Tony, 103
body politic, Adams on, 34–35
Brooks, Jennifer, 204n45
Brown, Ron, 104
Brown v. Board of Education, 146
Buckley, William F., 56
Bureau of Land Management, 61, 74
Bush, George W., 205n50
  address to nation after 9/11 attacks, 41
Bush Administration
  bailout, 119, 209n107

labor. *See also* child labor
  cheap, 105, 208n101
  Lincoln on, 36, 111
land. *See also* Bureau of Land Management; conservation
  privatization, 205n59
  publicly owned, 73–74, 186–87
  restoration, 186–87
Leopold, Aldo, 135–36
  on conservation, 129
Lewis and Clark, individualism myth and, 35
liberals, 73, 103, 150
  defined political label of, 197–98
  rights and responsibilities, 49–50
libertarian, 56, 204n47, 207n89
  defined political label of, 197
  extremist, 55
  free market, 110, 197, 207n89
Limbaugh, Rush, 70, 204n47
  on poverty, 158
Lincoln, Abraham, 5, 17, 24–25, 141, 175, 180
  on democracy, 106
  Gettysburg Address, 28, 33
  on labor and capital, 36, 111
  on slavery and pursuit of self-interest, 21
Lincoln-Douglas debates, 21, 25
living wage, 117, 169, 170
Liz Claiborne/Art Ortenberg Foundation, 95
local food systems, 139–40
Louisiana Purchase, 73, 120
Lovins, Amory, 138

Machine Age, 131
Madison, James, 87–88
Malkin, Michelle, 69
Manhattan Project, 188, 212n146
Mansfield, Mike, 188–89
Maoist China, 70
Marine Corps, 38–39
market
  competition, 102
  farmers', 139
  forces for conservation, 138–40
  global, 157
market values, 45, 47, 116, 134
  in education, 92–93

Marx, Karl, 72
Marxist socialism, 70, 210n119
  democratic socialism *vs.*, 72
  elimination of, 73
Massey Coal Company, 61, 204n43
Massey Energy safety violations, 36–37
McCain, John, 209n107
McCarthy, Joe, 73
"me"
  mindset, 51
  "we" and, balance between, 52, 54
media, 14, 40. *See also specific media*
  consolidation, 206n67
  consumer spending and, 41–42
  extreme Right, 68, 70
  under Hitler, 69
  manipulations, 44
  poverty and, 166–67
  reforms, 179–80, 184
  restoring responsible, 65–86
  socialism threat and, 70–77
  under Stalin, 70
Medicaid, 106
Medicare, 58, 75, 147–48, 164, 206n76
  as "socialist social engineering," 119
medicine. *See also* health care
  profit-driven, 211n143
  socialized, 75–76, 176
Mein Kampf (Hitler), 69
Mexican bank bailout, 30
Mickey Mouse, 42
Middle East, 31
Miles City, Montana, 14
military
  budget, 60
  recruitment slogan, 37–40
  as "socialist" institution, 74
  teamwork in, 38–39
Millennium Summit, UN, 190
minimum wage, federal, 166
  raising, 169–70
mining industry, 113–15
monopolies, control of, 102–3
Montana Heritage Project, 95
Montana Nature Conservancy, 116
Montana State University, 92–93
Moore, Bud, 38–39
moral compass, 175–76
moral virtues, 56
Morrill Act, 180

ABOUT THE AUTHOR

Brian Kahn has worked as a ranch hand, college boxing coach, lawyer, conservationist, journalist, and writer. He is host of the award-winning public radio program *Home Ground* and is the recipient of the 2009 Montana Governor's Award for the Humanities. He lives in Montana.

ABOUT SEVEN STORIES PRESS

Seven Stories Press is an independent book publisher based in New York City. We publish works of the imagination by such writers as Nelson Algren, Russell Banks, Octavia E. Butler, Ani DiFranco, Assia Djebar, Ariel Dorfman, Coco Fusco, Barry Gifford, Hwang Sok-yong, Lee Stringer, and Kurt Vonnegut, to name a few, together with political titles by voices of conscience, including the Boston Women's Health Collective, Noam Chomsky, Angela Y. Davis, Human Rights Watch, Derrick Jensen, Ralph Nader, Loretta Napoleoni, Gary Null, Project Censored, Barbara Seaman, Alice Walker, Gary Webb, and Howard Zinn, among many others. Seven Stories Press believes publishers have a special responsibility to defend free speech and human rights, and to celebrate the gifts of the human imagination, wherever we can. For additional information, visit www.sevenstories.com.